GREAT CYCLE JOURNEYS
OF THE WORLD

GREAT CYCLE JOURNEYS OF THE WORLD

NEW HOLLAND

First published in 2010 by
New Holland Publishers (UK) Ltd
London • Cape Town • Sydney • Auckland
www.newhollandpublishers.com

Garfield House
86–88 Edgware Road
London W2 2EA
United Kingdom

80 McKenzie Street
Cape Town 8001
South Africa

Unit 1, 66 Gibbes Street
Chatswood, NSW 2067
Australia

218 Lake Road
Northcote
Auckland
New Zealand

A catalogue record for this book is available from the British Library.

ISBN 978 1 84773 463 1

Senior Editor: Sarah Greaney
Designer: Isobel Gillan
Cartography: Stephen Dew
Production: Marion Storz
Publisher: Ross Hilton
Publishing Director: Rosemary Wilkinson

10 9 8 7 6 5 4 3 2 1

Reproduction by Pica Digital Pte Ltd, Singapore
Printed and bound by Tien Wah Press Pte Ltd, Singapore

The author and publishers have made every effort to ensure that all
information given in this book is accurate, but they cannot accept liability
for any resulting injury or loss or damage to either property or person,
whether direct or consequential and howsoever arising.

Page 1: The Grabouw region, approximately an hour's drive from Cape
Town, offers exceptional singletracking.
Pages 2–3: Snow dusts the amber rock landscape at the start of the
legendary Slickrock Trail in Moab, Utah.
Pages 4–5: A mountain biker crests the sea cliffs overlooking South
Africa's breathtaking Wild Coast.
Pages 6–7: Taking in a dramatic sunset within South Africa's arid
Northern Cape Province.

CONTENTS

INTRODUCTION

*"When I see an adult on a bicycle,
I do not despair for the future of the human race."*

H.G. WELLS

Leonardo da Vinci is widely, though somewhat controversially, credited with the invention of the bicycle. The infamous sketch that literary historian Augusto Marinoni sensationally claimed to have unearthed in 1974 during restoration work on da Vinci's *Codex Atlanticus* may, or may not, be a fake. What is certainly beyond dispute is the fact that in 1493, when the sketch was supposed to have been made, the engineering techniques to build such a contraption did not exist.

The world's first reliable bicycle was built in Baden, Germany, by Baron Karl von Drais in 1817. He called it a *Laufmaschine* or 'running machine', as it had no pedals and was propelled by the rider's feet like a scooter. He patented the design in 1818 and started making the 22 kg (49 lb) wooden contraptions, which soon became known as 'velocipedes'. News travelled fast, even in those days, and by the summer of 1819 Dennis Johnson was earning a good living in London selling his own version to the dandies of the town, for whom they were all the rage. Brakes had yet to be considered, and accidents were commonplace. This, combined with a hastily imposed £2 fine for their use on pavements, meant that this first wave of bicycle mania was short-lived.

Frenchman Pierre Lallement thought he had the answer. In 1863 he patented a bicycle with pedals and cranks directly connected to the front wheel hubs, and from 1867 the company Michaux et Cie manufactured what was to become famously known as the 'boneshaker'. This was still a pretty lethal machine. Lack of comfort notwithstanding, it had yet to address fundamentals such as changing direction and slowing down. Another Frenchman, Eugene Meyer, invented the wire-spoked tension wheel in 1869, and modified the boneshaker design to achieve higher speeds by simply increasing the size of the front wheel. Speed was thus effectively limited only by enthusiasm and the inside leg measurement of the owner, with front wheel diameters of up to 1.5 m (60 in) possible for the tallest riders. These machines became known as penny farthings in England and were notoriously unsafe. Fatalities were common with the rider travelling rapidly so far above the ground, and earthbound trajectories

▷ *A gnarly trail section near Hole-in-the-Wall, a natural rock arch along South Africa's rugged Eastern Cape coast.*

were long in the event of collisions. It was from such accidents that the expression 'come a cropper' – to land on one's head – entered the vernacular.

The man responsible for bringing this invention to the form we all recognize today was an Englishman called John Kemp Starley. In 1885 he patented the 'Rover', the world's first 'safety bicycle' complete with steerable front wheel and a chain-drive to the rear wheel. Thus began the cycling craze of the late Victorian era. By the mid 1890s Schoeninger's Western Wheel Works in Chicago was mass producing a model called the Crescent, and these affordable machines were being exported worldwide. Clubs proliferated, and as early as 1878 the Cycle Touring Club was founded as a national organization in England. The suffragettes were particularly enamored of the bicycle, both as an escape from domestic drudgery and a liberation from the constraints of 'acceptable' dress. Bloomers were invented for women to cycle in, a fact that caused considerable outrage amongst more conservative observers. As American feminist Susan Anthony wrote at the time, bicycling "has done more to emancipate women than anything else in the world. It gives women a feeling of freedom and self-reliance. I stand and rejoice every time I see a woman ride by on a wheel... the picture of free, untrammeled womanhood."

By the 1960s the bicycle had conquered the world. Exercise, fresh air and an escape at the end of the working week had people flocking to their local bike shops and out into the countryside. Sales doubled in America between 1960 and 1970, and then again by 1972, mostly of modern racing-type bikes with dropped handlebars, narrow tyres and derailleur gears. In China, meanwhile, the first of more than half a billion Flying Pigeon single-speed bikes emerged from the factory in Tienjin in 1954. It did not take long for some of the more masochistic and adventurous members of the cycling fraternity to realize that roads were cramping their style. The first Cyclo Cross world championship was held in 1950 in Paris, with Frenchmen securing the top three places, and the Roughstuff Fellowship was founded in England in 1955.

△ Wild riding along the high plateaus of South Africa's Baviaans River Valley.

It was in California, however, that the next big advance in bike technology was to happen – an advance that has redefined biking for many of us and allowed cyclists to become involved in the outdoors in a previously unimaginable way. In Marin County a group of young speed-freaks including seminal figures such as Tom Ritchey, Joe Breeze, Gary Fisher and Keith Bontrager were looking for thrills. On the forest firetrails of Mount Tamalpais they would hold downhill races, riding modified 1930s Schwinn Excelsior touring bikes with balloon tyres and motorbike handlebars – 'klunkers' – at breakneck speeds. The first custom 'mountain bike' was built by Joe Breeze in 1977, and by 1979 Gary Fisher and Charlie Kelly had founded their company and started producing the first models for sale. These cost $1,300 even then, and in their first year they produced just 160 bikes. The technology developed very rapidly, and five years later, in 1982, Specialized launched the Stumpjumper, a model that remains in production to this day.

Today, one may, if one's pocket is deep enough, spend thousands of pounds on a feather-light mountain bike with 24-speed gears, full suspension, disk brakes and a computer-designed carbon fibre frame. Without an appetite for excitement or *wanderlust*, such a machine is little more than a symbol of aspiration or wealth. Cycling has always attracted the eccentrics among us, the maverick adventurers prepared to think outside the box. Take Thomas Stevens, for example.

◁ The competitive element of mountain biking is a big draw for some.

Born in Hertfordshire, England, in 1854, he emigrated to California in 1872. Early in 1884 he acquired a 1.3 m (50 in) Columbia Standard penny farthing and, "seeking an adventure for his idle bravery", resolved to ride it around the world. No-one had succeeded in riding a bicycle across America at that time, let alone around the world, and our hero can scarcely have had any idea of what lay ahead as he blithely departed from San Francisco at 8am sharp on 22 April. In his handlebar bag were a spare shirt, several pairs of socks, a raincoat and a Smith & Wesson .38 revolver. One hundred and three-and-a-half days later he arrived in Boston. Twenty days stoppage for bad weather etc. *en route* meant that he had covered the 5,957 km (3,700 miles) of wagon road in just over eighty days, riding an average of 74 km (46 miles) a day. Many of us would be pleased with that figure on a modern bike and tarmac, but on a penny farthing and 19th century wagon roads it represents a considerable feat of athleticism! From New York he then sailed to Liverpool. Two-and-a-half years and 21,735 km (13,500 miles) later, at 10am on 17 December 1886, he finally vaulted from his saddle in front of the Club Hotel on the Yokohama bund, Japan.

More recently, Dervla Murphy has carried the torch for women adventurers. Born in 1931 and raised in Lismore, Ireland, she was given a bicycle and an atlas for her tenth birthday and within days had resolved to ride to India. In the midst of Britain's record storms and blizzards of 1963, she set off on her Armstrong Cadet bike and crossed to Dunkirk. Among the sundry items in her saddlebags were a large supply of cigarettes, and a pistol. One hundred and seventy-five days and 7,245 km (4,500 miles) later, she arrived in Delhi, having ridden through France, Italy, Yugoslavia, Turkey, Persia, Afghanistan and Pakistan. Her expenditure for the entire odyssey was just $175.

We may not all have the time or inclination to follow in the tracks of these indomitable bicycle pioneers, but if you have even the slightest propensity for two-wheeled excitement then the contents of this book will surely quicken your pulse. From Scotland to Slovenia, from New Zealand to Nepal, from Pakistan to the Pyrenees – wherever you are in the world, this cornucopia of cycling delights will have you reaching for your helmet and gloves.

◁ *Mountain bikers share the outback roads of the Augrabies National Park, RSA, with giraffe, eland, brown hyena and any number of poisonous snakes.*

▽ *Taking a breather outside a traditional shop in the erstwhile Transkei, now part of the Eastern Cape's Wild Coast.*

AFRICA

"After twenty-one days on the road I rode into Stanleyville on a blistering hot afternoon, endeavouring to assume an air of nonchalance, as though riding in from close by for an afternoon's shopping. The effect was rather spoilt when I fell off in the main street with the bicycle on top of me. I was very tired."

BILL TILMAN, CYCLING TO THE WEST COAST OF AFRICA IN SEPTEMBER 1932

△ *Stunning scenery at Pinnacle Point in South Africa.*

Kwame Nkrumah, the first president of independent Ghana, wrote that "I am an African, not because I was born in Africa but because Africa is born in me". No-one that has slept out under an African sky, savoured the smell of the first rains or heard a distant lion roar will disagree with that. There is, perhaps, nowhere on earth that quite matches the ability of this vast continent of contrast, contradiction and indescribable beauty to get under one's skin; to get into one's blood.

Africa is the world's second largest continent, covering an area in excess of 30 million square kilometres (11.7 million square miles) or 20 per cent of the earth's land. Over 75 per cent of this lies within the tropics. Mainland Africa contains 43 different countries with a combined population that will pass the billion mark by the year 2010. Over 1,000 languages are spoken by peoples whose ethnic diversity is unmatched anywhere else on earth. It was from here that *homo erectus* first ventured forth into the wider world some two million years ago, and to this day no other continent inspires such a sense of identity and belonging amongst those born or living there.

The sheer scale of Africa's geographical features is dizzying. The Nile is the longest river in the world, covering a staggering 6,650 km (4,135 miles). The Sahara is the biggest desert on earth, covering an area greater than that of the continental USA. Mount Kilimanjaro is both Africa's highest summit (5,895 m/19,340 ft) and the largest free-standing volcano on earth, with a base area that would cover the whole of greater London.

Coupled with the above geographical attractions, the continent's vast mineral and natural wealth has long attracted prospectors and explorers from the world over, many of them with motives a good deal less than altruistic. Names such as James Bruce, Mungo Park, Henry Morton Stanley and David Livingstone are part of the folklore of exploration, but can the same be said of Neil Clough?

This Mancunian geography teacher took it upon himself in 1978 to ride his bicycle to Cape Town. Setting off in August that year with several hundred pounds in cash and a ciné camera, it took him ten months and seventeen sets of tyres to cover the 16,140 km (10,029 miles) from Manchester to the Cape of Good Hope. In completing this journey he also became the first person to cross the Sahara with a bicycle. The choice of words is important here, as he did not actually *ride* his bike all the way. Fortunately for him, Herbert Kichener had built a railway from Wadi Halfa to Abu Hamed across the desert in the 1890s, and when riding the bike became impossible as his wheels sank into the sands, he balanced the rims on the railway track and pushed.

He touchingly recounts how, on his arrival at each maintenance station along the track, "the bike would be taken from my grasp and handled with the tenderness of a box of eggs. A stool would be placed beside the railway track and I would be courteously invited to sit down. A large aluminium bowl, filled with water, would be placed on the ground. Then one of the station crew would kneel in front of me, remove my trainers and wash my feet as if he was washing objects of bone china."

Riaan Manser from Cape Town went one better. In September 2003 he set out on his mountain bike to ride the whole way around the continent. Two years, two months and two days later he was back, having pedalled an incredible 36,500 km (22,680 miles) through 34 counties, lost 14 kg (31 lbs) in weight, learned French, Portuguese and Arabic, eaten monkeys, rats and bats and been kidnapped by child-soldiers in Liberia. The journeys described in the pages that follow may not be quite as epic, but they will certainly open your eyes to the wonders of this most wonderful of continents.

▽ *Ballistic singletrack in the High Atlas, Morocco.*

MOROCCO
The Atlas Traverse

STEVE RAZZETTI

Paul Bowles wrote that "If people and their manner of living were alike everywhere, there would not be much point in moving from one place to another." There can be few places on earth from where one has to travel such a small distance to experience such a profound cultural shift as south across the Straits of Gibraltar from Tarifa in Spain. Just 13 km (8 miles) of water separate the resort-strewn coast of Andalucia, with its luxury villas, motorways, boutique-lined harbours and throbbing night clubs, from the dusty *souks* and ancient *casbahs* of Morocco.

Inland from the Spanish coast lie the *Pueblos Blancos* ('White Towns') and the fabulously rugged Sierra Nevada, whilst travelling south away from the sea in Morocco one is soon

▽ *A dead tree above Magdaz.*

confronted by an even more spectacular range of mountains, the Atlas. Stretching in an arc across Maghreb in northern Africa, they span a distance of over 2,400 km (1,500 miles) from Tunisia in the east, through Algeria and to within a few miles of Agadir and the Atlantic in southwest Morocco. These are the Himalaya of Africa, whose orogenesis began in the Palaeozoic era, some 300 million years ago. Incredible as it may seem, these mountains are thought to have been formed before the Atlantic Ocean separated Africa from America, by the same tectonic event that created the Appalachians in the eastern USA.

The High Atlas, culminating in the summit of Djebel Toubkal (4,167 m/13,671 ft) lie at the western end of the range, and the summits are snowbound for all but a few weeks of the year. The entire Atlas is a very barren range, but like all mountains close to oceans, they capture what little moisture does drift onshore from the Mediterranean and oblige it to precipitate on their northern slopes. Here you will find cedar, thuya and juniper clinging on in sheltered, watered valleys. The arid southern flanks descend into the Sahara and can be fiercely hot in summer.

Many find the scenery reminiscent of Central Asia – indeed, Martin Scorcese used the village of Imlil and the vicinity below Toubkal as locations during the filming of his epic *Kun Dun*, about the Dalai Lama of Tibet. The reality, however, is that the Atlas are home to an ancient Berber architecture and culture that is quite unique. References to their presence throughout Maghreb abound in records from ancient Egypt, Greece and the Roman empire, though today they have largely been assimilated into Arab society. Only amongst the mountains of the Atlas does their culture survive intact, and this is a large part of the attraction of the region.

Access to the Atlas for visitors arriving from abroad is usually gained via Marrakesh. Also known as Al Hamra ('The Red City'), its airport is served by various budget airlines and is only a three hour flight from most northern European cities. Set in the foothills on the north of the range, it is an exquisitely exotic place, complete with a spectacular *medina* or walled city, within the precincts of which is the largest *souk* in Morocco and the famous Djemaa el Fna square. By day this is a thronging and colourful melée of hustlers, storytellers, water-sellers and acrobats, but after dusk it is transformed into a vast open-air restaurant, complete with serenading musicians, flamboyant stall holders and the infamous ladies of the night.

△ *Riding the awesome singletrack descent from the Tizi-n-Rouguelt towards Ichbbakene.*

△ *Telouet Casbah.*

△ ABOVE RIGHT *Resting after the tarmac road-climb to the Tizi-n-Tichka from Telouet.*

▷ *Riding across the Yagour Plateau at around 2,000 m (6,560 ft).*

▽ OVERLEAF *Looking at the road up to the Tizi-n-Imlil from above Ouaneskra village.*

Biking in the High Atlas presents a real challenge, and this is probably the toughest route described in this book. Gentler rides are to be found in the Anti Atlas and Jbel Sarho in the southwest of the country, but the traverse of the High Atlas is a technically challenging, fat-tyre adventure that will really test your riding skills. Most of the route – 80 per cent – is on piste dirt roads or singletrack paths between villages, and will have to be ridden unsupported. You will need to arrange to have your luggage transferred to your overnight stops, which will vary from comfortable gîtes and Berber houses to bivouacs, by vehicle or mule. Carrying your own kit on your bike is not feasible on a route with so many technical sections to negotiate, and even the most proficient riders will find themselves carrying their bikes both up and down some of the more treacherous stretches of trail.

From cruising the fertile and scenically stunning Ayt Bou Wgemmaz valley, with irrigated fields set like glistening emeralds amid the barren mountains and village clusters of distinctive flat-roofed *pisé* (mud) houses, to the blazing singletrack descent into the Tessaout gorge from Tizi-n-Rouguelt (a pass at 2,860 m/9,385 ft), this is a mountain bike journey in the purest sense. Away from roads and through the heart of the mountains – wild, sustained and completely unforgettable.

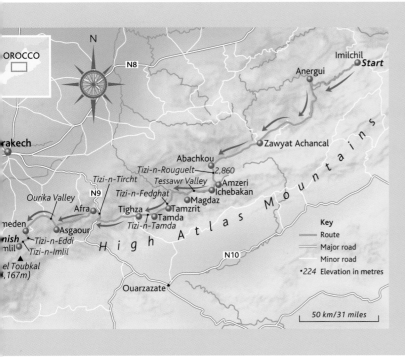

DESCRIPTION: A technically challenging and physically demanding traverse of the High Atlas in Morocco.

ROUTE LENGTH AND DURATION: Roughly 650 km (400 miles). Can be ridden in 10 days, but longer is recommended to allow for rest days and side trips.

WHEN TO GO: May/June and September/October – avoid the summer heat.

SPECIAL CONSIDERATIONS: Mid- to high-spec mountain bike recommended (fully serviced) and a decent spares kit. You will be spending entire days away from support vehicles, so think about spares/tools to be carried and ride carefully. If your bike has hydraulic brakes/suspension make sure you know how it works. Mobile phone cover in the Atlas is generally fairly good. Carry plenty of water and avoid heatstroke.

TOUR OPERATORS: KE Adventure Travel (www.keadventure.com) pioneered this route. In Morocco, support vehicles and other logistics can be arranged through ERG Tours (www.ergtours.com).

BOTSWANA
The Mashatu Game Reserve

JACQUES MARAIS

▽ *Guides are always on hand for support and advice on biking in this extraordinary landscape.*

Travel north from South Africa to beyond the muddy roil of the Limpopo River, and you will discover a patch of big-sky country where you may cruise endless game tracks while tipping your cycling helmet to a passing parade of pachyderm. Botswana is the archetypal 'Africa for Beginners' destination, and visitors will revel in landscapes ranging from wetland swamps to windswept desert dunes.

For a truly wild ride, head into the Tuli Block, a vast wilderness area hunkering down against its border with Zimbabwe and South Africa. Here, in the Mashatu Game Reserve, you will saddle up in the shadow of ancient baobabs gracing an uncluttered skyline, and ride like the wind while thundershowers march in across the endless plains.

Situated within the eastern sliver of Botswana, the 26,000 ha (64,220 acre) Mashatu Game Reserve encompasses a jumble of arid plains, sandy river beds and rocky outcrops. Craggy kloofs and ridges, dense with straggly stands of scotia-, mopane- and knob-thorn trees, are home to the legendary Shashe herds, currently Africa's largest elephant population on private land. Well over 700 of these lumbering giants still share this section of the Tuli Block with lion, leopard, cheetah, spotted hyena, giraffe, eland, wildebeest and other mammals, as well as with a dazzling selection of birds and reptiles.

This is one of only a handful of southern African Big Five reserves offering mountain biking as an adventure activity. Mashatu therefore regularly lures off-road riders from around the globe, and most of them come here with one mission in mind: to face off with an elephant across the handlebars of their bike. And the beauty of Mashatu's mountain bike trails is that you can tailor-make the ride to suit you and your group's level of fitness and experience.

Generally, day one will see you arriving at the Pont Drift border post at around midday. Once you have dealt with the border formalities, it is time to get your bikes and the support vehicles ready, and then hit the road to the first wilderness camp, the location of which will vary depending on the route you take. Although the camps are low-impact and

△ *Riders inspect a lion kill along the Mashatu mountain biking trail.*

△ ABOVE LEFT *Loading the mountain bikes after an exploratory ride on day one.*

DESCRIPTION: A four day mountain bike ride, mostly along elephant trails and game tracks, in a Big Five Game Reserve. The ride is rated moderate to difficult.

ROUTE LENGTH AND DURATION: Daily legs vary from 25–45 km (16–28 miles); you should be relatively fit.

WHEN TO GO: All year, but summer (October–January) is extremely hot, with thunderstorm activity.

SPECIAL CONSIDERATIONS: Thorn-proofing (go for both sealant and tyre liners) is a necessity. Equipment-wise, a good quality mountain bike, riding apparel and basic spares are needed. There are no bike shops even remotely near Mashatu, so plan accordingly. Helmets are compulsory. Bikes are available for hire, but bring your own pedals and shoes.

MAPS: Not required, as all rides are guided.

TOUR OPERATORS: www.cyclemashatu.co.za

PERMITS/RESTRICTIONS: Cycle Mashatu are the only operator allowed to run trips here. Passports are required, and check whether you need a visa to enter Botswana from South Africa.

ACCOMMODATION: Wilderness accommodation is included as part of the adventure package.

environmentally friendly, they are comfortable enough to ensure an unforgettable night in the bush. Bucket showers, chilled drinks and meals prepared over an open fire will be just the ticket after a hard day's ride.

Freshly brewed coffee and the sounds of a savannah dawn will tempt you out of your camp cot on day two. Routes vary depending on group ability, but you can expect to spend around five hours in the saddle and cover 25–45 km (16–28 miles) per day. Most of the riding is along game tracks and, as the animals stick to natural contours, you can expect a gloriously undulating crank. The second night's stopping place is again a temporary camp, and a leisurely siesta will recharge your batteries before a late afternoon outing to the nearby sundowner viewpoint.

Basalt extrusions mean stony and rocky terrain, but be warned, you will encounter sand every now and then, especially in the lower-lying areas of the reserve. Expect to crank hard through dry river beds, or when ascending the rocky kopjes. Drainage lines and the corresponding gnarly drop-offs will test you, especially along the ride to Kgotla Camp on day three, but the lure of hot showers and a sumptuous pasta lunch are sure to keep your legs going. And if that doesn't, the knowledge that leopard and lion may be lurking close by will. Although the big cats usually take flight, close encounters with elephants and other big game are virtually guaranteed. Elephants obviously present the biggest challenge while riding in Mashatu, especially along wooded sections of the trail. The guides, although armed, have yet to fire a shot on an outride, and instead use their extensive wilderness knowledge to ensure a safe distance between riders and animals.

On your final day, you can opt to return to Pont Drift by either vehicle or bike, or you may just decide to end your adventure within the luxurious surrounds of Mashatu's premium tented camp. Add-on days within the reserve may be arranged to follow on from your mountain biking adventure, thus allowing you to experience the wildlife on day and night drives. The time will come when you eventually have to say goodbye to this antediluvian land, but until then, take every opportunity to drink in the timelessness of this profound and beautiful place.

◁ *One of the Mashatu matriarchs slaking her thirst at a water hole.*

▽ *Armed rangers accompany you on all outrides within the Mashatu Game Reserve.*

SOUTH AFRICA
The Western Cape

JACQUES MARAIS

▽ *Cyclists relax along the False Bay coastline near Simonstown before cranking into the Smitswinkel climb towards Cape Point Nature Reserve gate.*

Adventure awaits you at the southern tip of the African continent. Here, along a narrow spit of land known as the Cape of Storms, the global outdoor tribe is discovering a historic city where the cosmopolitan spirit of Europe rushes headlong into traditional African culture. And once you've had your urban fix, saddle up and head beyond the funky Cape Town streets to where the legendary Table Mountain National Park unfolds along the rugged peninsula.

Cranking the Cape Peninsula can be done either as a multi-day tour, or may be conveniently broken up into a few individual stages. The latter option offers more freedom, and also allows you to savour both the on- and off-road flavours of the Cape.

On day one, heed the calling of the tarmac curves meandering south from Cape Town. The 109 km (68 mile) circular route from the city centre traverses the tempestuous Atlantic coastline, dipping and climbing through sleepy fishing villages slumbering within the shadow of Table Mountain. The foothills of this renowned granitic range are blanketed in *fynbos* (fine bush) vegetation, a blend of protea, erica and restios heathers shaping the richest botanical ecosystem on the planet.

Your ride will follow the route of the Argus Cycle Tour, the world's biggest individually timed sporting event. Every year, approximately 35,000 riders set off from Green Point, cycling in a spandex frenzy via Cape Town's southern suburbs towards Muizenberg. From here, they trace the rocky coastline through Kalk Bay, Fish Hoek and the historic Simonstown before ascending towards Cape Point Nature Reserve.

Pass the curio sellers and an ostrich farm, working the back section before dropping down to remote Scarborough and ethereal Misty Cliffs. Take in the gorgeous views, then blast through Kommetjie and Noordhoek onto Chapmans Peak, undoubtedly the *pièce de resistance* of the ride. For 10 km (6 miles), you will flatline the phenomenal road to Hout Bay, overdosing on heady views while cliffs plummet hundreds of metres into the aquamarine ocean far below.

△ *A high vantage point shows riders streaming along the Argus Cycle Tour route, the world's biggest timed sporting event.*

The calf-crunching Suikerbossie climb lurks next. And then it's just you and the wind in your hair, as you zigzag back into town via glorious Camps Bay. This is an eminently achievable ride even though you are looking at more than 100 km (62 miles) in the saddle, and fairly fit cyclists should complete the route in anything between 4–8 hours.

Day two, and it's time to hit the dirt. Now that you've explored the coastline of the Cape Peninsula, you need to head inland and bang into the mountains. Two mountain bike routes stand out in Cape Town's immediate vicinity. Right above the City Bowl, a network of jeep tracks criss-cross the eastern face of Table Mountain, ripping from Deer Park through to the Rhodes Memorial. This constitutes approximately 30 km (19 miles) of riding, with stunning views of Table Bay across the city.

▽ A downhill rider gets big air along the Deer Park section of the Table Mountain range.

True fat-tyre freaks will trek south in search of the singletrack paradise that is Tokai Forest. Blood, sweat and granny gears will be the order of the day as you wind your way up 12 km (7 miles) of steep jeep track to the radio mast above Elephant's Eye Cave, but the fun really kicks in once you head onto the downhill trails. A range of trail configurations are possible in Tokai, which is part working plantation and part indigenous forest. The trailhead starts at the Arboretum, and from here a gruelling stretch of gravel road snakes up into the rugged Table Mountain range. It is possible to link through into Silvermine Nature Reserve to extend your ride, and the good news is that it will be downhill all the way from there.

A number of singletrack options, varying from white-knuckle downhill drops to side-winding berms, now wait to take you back down to the Arboretum. Route choices vary depending on any tree-felling taking place, so it might take you a while to discover all the nooks and crannies. And while you crank your way through this emerald wonderland, keep an eye out for lynx, porcupine, Cape grysbok (a tiny mountain gazelle) and the resident chacma baboon troop.

Off-the-bike leisure and action options are sure to blow your mind as well. Cosmopolitan Cape Town currently rates as one of the hottest tourist destinations on the planet, and visitors flock here from around the world. A good infrastructure, breathtaking natural splendour, affordable prices and an exhilarating nightlife make this a city with something to suit every taste. There are beaches galore: surf at Muizenberg or Kommetjie, go horse riding on Noordhoek, cool off at Camps Bay or join the body beautiful brigade at Clifton to soak up the sun.

Otherwise, venture into the adrenaline zone to see why the Cape is fast becoming the world's most popular adventure destination. Abseil 112 m (367 ft) off the top of Table Mountain, rock climb the heady granite slopes or, if that is not extreme enough, paraglide from the top of Lion's Head. Microlighting, hang-gliding, canyoning, shark diving, sandboarding, caving, big wave surfing and kiteboarding are just a few of the extreme sport angles to explore.

It is not necessary to be an adrenaline junkie to enjoy nature, though. The whole of Cape Town is ensconced within a world-renowned national park, and leisure options are a dime a dozen. Snorkel with African penguins at Boulder's Beach, sea kayak the False Bay coastline, go for a gentle stroll in Kirstenbosch Botanical Gardens or glide to the top of Table Mountain in the revolving cable car. There's really no other place quite like it.

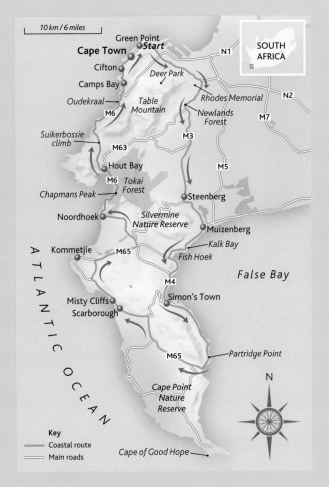

facts and figures

DESCRIPTION: Two distinctive day rides, one on tarmac and one on dirt.

ROUTE LENGTH AND DURATION: Tarmac – 109 km (68 miles), circular, 4–8 hours; off-road – approx. 30 km (19 miles), various configurations, 2–5 hours.

WHEN TO GO: September through to May.

SPECIAL CONSIDERATIONS: Bikes may be hired from various operators in Cape Town. On tarmac you'll need a hybrid or road bike; off-road you'll need a full-suspension mountain bike.

MAPS: Tarmac – city centre; off-road – Tokai Arboretum.

TOUR OPERATORS: Tarmac – www.bike&saddle.com; off-road – www.downhilladventures.com.

PERMITS/RESTRICTIONS: Tarmac – public roads; off-road – permit available at Tokai entrance.

ACCOMMODATION: Book on www.tourismcapetown.co.za or www.capepointroute.co.za.

ASIA

"It is by riding a bicycle that you learn the contours of a country best, since you have to sweat up the hills and coast down them... you have no such accurate remembrance of a country you have driven through as you gain by riding a bicycle."

ERNEST HEMINGWAY

△ Essential maintenance at the end of the day in Tingri, Tibet.

In Asia, one colossal geographical fact makes these words of Hemingway all the more apposite: the Himalaya. Nowhere else are there so many contour lines so close together. Mythical, mysterious, and above all, jaw-droppingly beautiful, the highest range of mountains on earth has shaped the culture, economics and history of an entire continent almost since the beginning of time.

Forming a fearsome mountain barrier across the entire northern boundary of the Indian subcontinent, the perpetually snow-clad summits of the Himalaya have acted as a natural geographic and political frontier, a divine inspiration for mystics and philosophers, and at the same time arrested the northerly progress of summer monsoon clouds from the Bay of Bengal. Forced to rise in their vain attempts to pass over them, these clouds are obliged to precipitate their torrential rains onto the southern slopes, feeding tumultuous rivers, irrigating rice paddies, giving life to millions of people and sustaining spectacularly diverse ecosystems.

To the north, in the biggest rain-shadow on earth, the endless upland deserts and steppes of Tibet and Central Asia languish in almost total drought. Here one may find aquatic fossils in ancient sedimentary deposits that have been elevated from the seabed to altitudes in excess of 5,000 m (16,400 ft) by the tectonic forces of India's ongoing collision with Asia.

For travellers, all this has many implications. Even during high summer, the winds that tear across the Tibetan plateau can be bitingly cold and desiccating, while during the deepest winter, the Alpine zone and its glaciers may be buried under driving snow when just a few kilometres to the south and several thousand metres below, the valley floors are still swelteringly warm and humid.

Culturally, the diversity of this region is as pronounced as it is geographically. One may take salt and butter tea with a Buddhist monk in his freezing monastic cell at the beginning of a ride, and share a *chillum* with a loin-cloth clad dreadlocked Hindu *saddhu* beneath a banyan tree at the end. One may sip imported champagne in a hotel bar in the evening, and fermented mare's milk in the tent of a nomad the following afternoon.

While it is certainly true that the most intimate knowledge of a landscape is acquired by walking through it, the advent of road transport in the Himalaya has opened a fantastic range of opportunities to those who subscribe to the 'two wheels good, four wheels bad' ethos. The meanings of previously innocuous phrases such as 'long climb' or 'screaming descent' are elevated to new levels of seriousness here, where one may cross a bitterly cold pass at 5,000 m (16,400 ft) in the morning, enjoy an adrenaline-fuelled 60 km (37 mile) switchback downhill speed-fest, and dismount a short while later with one's ears popping to relax in the delicious shade of a jungle tree.

It is an understatement to say that Asia is big continent. The roads and tracks featured in the pages that follow are often rough, frequently blocked, traffic-free and far from what we call civilization. These are big trips, requiring a degree of fitness on the part of the rider, a level of mechanical preparedness on the part of the bike, and a generous dose of what we might euphemistically call a spirit of adventure.

▽ *Ogling the peaks of Hunza from the Karakoram Highway in Pakistan.*

CENTRAL ASIA
Almaty to Gilgit

STEVE RAZZETTI

The interminable trackless steppes and lonely mountains of Central Asia have been crossed by intrepid souls from far and wide since time immemorial. Two thousand years ago the Chinese traveller Syuan Tzam reached Lake Issyk-Kul in what is Kyrgyzstan today, crossing the Tien Shan on his way. Of this range he wrote, "Snow accumulating here from the beginning of the world has reduced to ice blocks which thaw neither in spring, nor in summer. Smooth fields of firm and bright ice stretch in boundlessness by high ice walls hanging from both sides. The cold wind blows with force, and travellers often become victims of dragons. Travellers going by this road should not let out loud cries. The one who forgets this precaution can undergo different misfortunes." Thirteen of his fellow travellers perished during this journey.

▽ *Climbing from Batan into the valley of the Oyzhaylau River on the first day's ride.*

Perhaps Petr Petrovich Semyenov had not read of this. The distinguished Russian geographer survived two expeditions to the Tien Shan – in 1856 and 1857 – during which he both determined that Issyk-Kul has no outlet and became the first European to set eyes on the peak which is now universally accepted as the most beautiful in the range, the magnificent Khan Tengri (7,010 m/22,993 ft).

The Tien Shan, or 'Celestial Mountains', form an arc over 2,800 km (1,736 miles) long stretching northeastwards from the Pamirs and the Hindu Kush along the border between Chinese Xinjiang and Kazakhstan/Kyrgyzstan. Essentially they form the mountainous northern rim of the Takla Makhan desert. Khan Tengri was long thought to be the highest peak in the range, but a Russian survey in 1946 found that the height of nearby Jengish Chokusu or Pik Pobedy ('Victory Peak') was in fact 7,439 m (24,400 ft). They are the most northerly 7,000 m (22,960 ft) peaks in the world.

Crossing the Kungey Alatau range from Almaty to Lake Issyk Kul gives spectacular panoramas of these peaks. This part of the journey is mostly on disused Soviet jeep tracks built to facilitate border patrols, when this was the frontier between the Russian and Chinese empires. Today they are completely devoid of traffic and perfect for mountain bikes. Issyk Kul is the second-largest saline lake in the world after the Caspian Sea, and is 195 km (121 miles) long and 700 m (2,296 ft) deep. Russian archaeologists and divers recently discovered a city dating from before 500 BC on the bed of the lake and have retrieved many sensational artifacts.

The route from here into Chinese Xinjiang is via Naryn and the Torugart Pass. This is on marginally better roads and the distances are huge. From Issyk Kul to Naryn is 395 km (245 miles) and it's then another 140 km (87 miles) to the Torugart Pass and the Chinese border, across largely empty but incredibly beautiful steppes. The only signs of human life you are likely to see on this stretch are the distant yurt encampments of Kyrgyz nomads and the occasional heavily overloaded Lada careering by at breakneck speed. If you have a decent map or a local guide, be sure to make the short detour and visit the beautifully preserved medieval *caravanserai* at Tash Rabat. Nomads have set up a permanent camp

△ *Camping by the Assy River on the first night.*

facts and figures

DESCRIPTION: A two-wheeled odyssey crossing the Kungey Alatau and Tien Shan ranges into Chinese Xinjiang and thence south across the Khunjerab Pass into Pakistan.

ROUTE LENGTH AND DURATION: 1,475 km (915 miles), ± 483 km (300 miles) off-road in Kyrgyzstan, ± 25 days.

WHEN TO GO: August–September.

SPECIAL CONSIDERATIONS: Central Asian dust + oil = a very efficient grinding paste – a self-cleaning wax lube is strongly recommended. Carry tools and spares and ensure that you can maintain your bike. If you do any of this trip unsupported, carry warm bivuoac gear and food.

TOUR OPERATORS: This route was pioneered by Glenn Rowley of KE Adventure Travel (www.keadventure.com). Recommended local agents are Khan Tengri in Almaty, Kazakhstan (www.kantengri.kz/index1.html) and the Celestial Mountains Tour Company in Bishkek, Kyrgyzstan (www.celestial.com.kg).

PERMITS/RESTRICTIONS: The crux of this trip is the Torugart Pass, which is technically closed to foreigners. Obtain permission to cross from the Chinese Department of Foreign Affairs in Urumchi (Xinjiang), and your Chinese tour company must meet you at the pass. 'No man's land' covers over 100 km (62 miles), and you are not allowed to ride this section. Even if you want to do the rest of the trip independently you will need Kyrgyz and Chinese agents to organize your crossing of this remote pass.

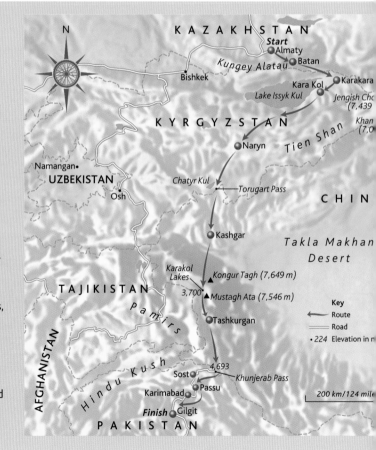

here and accommodation can be arranged. Nearer the pass, marvel at the intense blue colour of Chatyr Kul Lake. This is another body of saline water, with seven rivers draining into it and no outlet. Migrating birds pause here during the summer, but as you shelter from the wind in the scorching sun, imagine the place in winter – temperatures drop below -50°C (-58°F).

Once in Xinjiang the roads improve marginally again, and the 350 km (217 mile) journey from Kashgar up to the Khunjerab Pass via Tashkurgan is sensational. Be sure to overnight at Karakol Lakes (3,700 m/12,136 ft) – this is one of the most beautiful places in Chinese Turkestan and a wonderful finale to the Central Asian part of this odyssey. Above the sparkling blue waters of the lakes rise the enormous, brooding, snow-clad bulks of Mustagh Ata (7,546 m/24,752 ft) and Kongur Tagh (7,649 m/25,089 ft), and as you stand in the doorway of a yurt sipping tea and sheltering from that ever-present wind, you may wonder what on earth drove the Swedish explorer Sven Hedin to attempt to ride a yak to the summit of the former in 1894.

The contrast, as you descend into Pakistan from the Khunjerab Pass, is complete. Suddenly the valleys are steep and lined with verdant, irrigated orchards and picturesque villages. Gone are the vast, windswept steppes and impossibly distant horizons, replaced by precipitous rocky gorges, awesome mountains so steep and rugged that snow can barely cling to them, and oases of tranquil shade where you may sit and eat apricots and wonder at the audacity of the journey you have just made.

△ *Riding through the Karkara valley in the foothills of the Tien Shan.*

◁ FAR LEFT *A Kyrgyz boy on horseback at At Bashy.*

◁ NEAR LEFT *The felt door of a Kyrgyz yurt at At Bashy.*

▽ OVERLEAF *Lake Chatyr Kul, near the Torugart Pass.*

PAKISTAN
Hunza to Chitral

STEVE RAZZETTI

▷ *Biking the recently completed jeep road to Shimshal.*

▽ *Pausing at the excellent Passu Inn.*

In 1978, after a 20 year engineering and building marathon during which 15,000 Pakistanis and 30,000 Chinese toiled away in conditions of almost unimaginable danger and hardship, a ribbon was snipped at the 4,733 m (15,524 ft) Khunjerab Pass, and the Karakoram Highway (KKH) declared open. Snaking for 1,300 km (806 miles) from Kashgar in China's Xinjiang province to the Pakistani capital Islamabad, this wonder of the road-makers' craft crosses the highest frontier in the world and for much of its length hugs the banks of the mighty Indus River. The enormous defile through which this river flows separates the Karakoram range from the Himalaya, and is one of the most seismically active areas on earth. These are geologically young mountains, whose summits are still being pushed skyward by the tectonic forces of the Indian subcontinent's collision with Asia. Keeping the KKH open in the face of perpetual earthquakes and landslides requires a force of several thousand men, and the road itself is a memorial to the 900 souls who perished during its construction.

Purists may feel drawn to the challenge of a ride along the entire length of the KKH, but in truth the Chinese section and that below Gilgit in Pakistan are of less interest to mountain bikers. Increasing volumes of traffic, desert winds in China and searing heat in Indus Kohistan all conspire to make these stretches arduous in the extreme. For those in search of a more technically challenging and traffic-free ride, the 258 km (160 mile) ride down the KKH along the Hunza Valley from Khunjerab to Gilgit can be continued with the challenging 406 km (252 mile) crossing of the Shandur Pass (3,734 m/12,248 ft) into neighbouring Chitral and the mountains of the Hindu Kush.

From Khunjerab to Gilgit the KKH descends 3,200 m (10,496 ft) through mountain scenery described by the British explorer Eric Shipton as "the ultimate manifestation of mountain grandeur." It would be possible to complete this journey in three days on a bike, but in doing so one would miss the secrets hidden in the many side valleys that penetrate the mountains on either side of the highway. Day trips or longer into the valleys of Chapursan, Shimshal and Nagar all provide unbelievably spectacular and challenging rides

△ *Riding in the Ghizer Valley out of Gilgit towards Chitral.*

▷ FAR RIGHT *Idyllic riverside camping in the Ghizer Valley near Singul.*

on rough jeep roads and give a true flavour of the delights of Hunza away from the main highway. The old 'road' from the days before the KKH can also be spotted and followed by more technically proficient (brave!) riders in several places. A day or two savouring the delights of Karimabad are also highly recommended: apricots, mulberries, local wine, a charmingly relaxed and bucolic atmosphere and sensational views of Rakaposhi (7,788 m/ 25,545 ft) and Ultar (7,388 m/24,233 ft) are your reward. Hunzakuts are Ishmaili Muslims and signs of the Aga Khan's munificence abound, from the modern girls' college to irrigation schemes, from the carefully restored hilltop fort to experimental bio-gas plants. The town, previously known as Baltit, was in fact renamed Karimabad after the current Aga Khan, Prince Karim al-Hussaini.

Arriving in Gilgit any time between April and September, you may be glad you opted for the more mountainous journey onwards to Chitral. The town nestles in a broad valley and the sweltering summer heat here is but a foretaste to that which awaits the traveller in places such as Chilas and Besham further south. Temperatures in the upper 40s celcius (115°F-plus) are common, even in Gilgit. Better to relax a while in the shade of the chinar trees by Gilgit's rushing river, and then turn west toward the Hindu Kush.

In a hurry, one could ride over the Shandur from Gilgit to Chitral in five days, but, as in Hunza, the direct route is best taken as a thread upon which a number of exciting side-trips and diversions can be woven according to time available and sense of adventure. The tarmac doesn't last long upon leaving Gilgit, and the road to Chitral soon degenerates

DESCRIPTION: A road tour – mostly rough tarmac and unmetalled jeep track – of northern Pakistan, featuring a descent of the Hunza valley on the Karakoram Highway, and a crossing of the Shandur Pass into Chitral.

ROUTE LENGTH AND DURATION: 665 km (412 miles), ± 14 days biking.

WHEN TO GO: April–October, but expect snow at higher elevations until mid-May.

SPECIAL CONSIDERATIONS: High-spec mountain bike recommended, plus support vehicle(s) and camping equipment. Mountain bike parts are unavailable anywhere in Pakistan. Do not wear lycra in Islamic countries! Carry plenty of treated water – dehydration is a real issue here.

MAPS: AMS 'U–502' series, sheet no. NJ-43-15, 'Shimshal' and sheet no. NJ-43-14 'Baltit'. Also the Swiss 1990 1:250,000, Karakoram sheets one and two.

TOUR OPERATORS: Very few foreign agencies still work here. KE Adventure Travel (www.keadventure.com) in the UK are a good first choice. In Pakistan contact Nazir Sabir Expeditions (www.nazirsabir.com) or Hindu Kush Trails (www.hindukushtrails.com).

ACCOMMODATION: Hotel and hostel accommodation is available in the larger villages in Hunza, but tents and camping equipment will be required between Gilgit and Chitral.

into a rough jeep track and winds its way up the Gilgit and Ghizar river valleys. To the south, across a range of barren mountains, lie the Indus Valley and Kohistan. To the north, jeep tracks lead off into the wonderfully picturesque districts of Ishkoman and Yasin, where another week could easily be spent exploring on your bike. The urge to leave your bike a while here and trek off into the higher valleys may well prove irresistible.

Time your journey right, and you may be able to witness the raucous jamboree that accompanies the annual Gilgit vs Chitral polo tournament, which takes place on the crest of the Shandur Pass. Horses, riders and supporters walk from their respective sides in order to acclimatize for the rigours of high altitude polo. Competition is intense and spirits run high.

The 60 km (37 mile) downhill from Shandur to Mastuj is as ballistic as anything so far encountered, and from this oasis in the Chitral Valley you may continue south to Chitral town, or turn north into the Yarkhun Valley and ride to within a few kilometres of the border with Afghanistan.

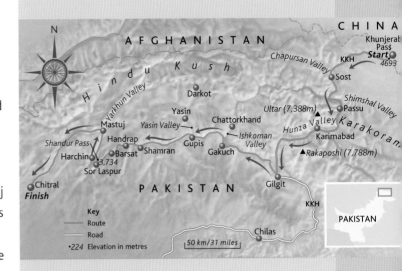

41

INDIA
Leh to Manali

STEVE RAZZETTI

▽ *On the descent from the Kardung La to Leh, with the Indus Valley beyond.*

François Bernier, French physician to the Mughal emporer Aurangzeb, was the first European to set foot in Kashmir. Writing in 1665, he said, "In truth, the kingdom surpasses in beauty all that my warmest imagination had anticipated." Long a favourite summer haunt of the British Raj, it was from the idyllic *chinar*-lined canals and water gardens of the capital, Srinagar, that the Indians built the road into neighbouring Ladakh – the 434 km (270 mile) Beacon Highway.

Few of earth's paradises have suffered the ravages of recent history more than this tiny corner of heaven in the Himalaya. Post-partition squabbles between India and Pakistan have never been far below the surface, and the fact that the Beacon Highway passes so close to the Line of Control between the two countries has meant that it has always been at best a tenuous link. Add to this the fact that for seven months every year the high passes are under snow, and the precariousness of Ladakh's lifeline can be appreciated. Domestic turmoil in northern India in the late 1980s further saw to it that Kashmir – and the road to Ladakh – sank below the radar of travellers, plunging the area into economic decline. In 1990, 600,000 Indian and 60,000 foreign tourists visited Kashmir and Ladakh. By 1992 that figure had plunged to 5,000 in total.

The strategic importance of Ladakh to the Indians cannot be overestimated. The capital, Leh, sits in the wide valley of the Indus River at an altitude of 3,505 m (11,496 ft), and has for centuries been an important staging post on the Silk Route. Today the old town, dominated by the Potala-like palace of the Ladakhi royal family, has been surrounded on all sides by the sprawling garrisons of the Indian army. There is an airport close by, but with mountain weather so fickle it is upon land links that the town ultimately depends.

It was for these reasons that, in 1989, the Indian authorities opened the previously out of bounds military route from Manali to Leh to foreigners. Now known as National Highway 1B, this 470 km (291 mile) 'road' is even more rugged and difficult than the famous Beacon Highway. The passes are more numerous and higher, and much of the surface has only recently been engineered to resemble anything close to what most people would call a road. Those travelling this way can but wonder at the tenacity of the Border Roads Organization, and Project HIMANK, whose men are charged with keeping it open.

Few mountain bike journeys are as challenging. As if the actual Leh to Manali ride was not enough, sensible folk will want to spend up to a week in the vicinity of Leh, acclimatizing to the altitude before heading south. The first of five passes on the journey is the 5,280 m (17,318 ft) Taglang La – the second highest road pass in the world. By planning your acclimatization rides around Leh carefully, you can make this a hat-trick of the three highest passes by riding up and descending back from the Kardung La (5,380 m/ 17,646 ft) and the Wari La (5,159 m/16,922 ft) – both routes north from the Indus Valley into the fabled Nubra.

If you are fit, have acclimatized sufficiently and are lucky with the condition of the road, notwithstanding breakdowns the ride to Manali from Leh will take a week. There is almost nothing in the way of accommodation available on the way, so a support vehicle and camping equipment is strongly recommended. This will enable you to choose your

▽ *Bikers at the Kardung La/Nubra sign at the road junction in Leh.*

own overnight stops and sample the wilderness you are riding through more completely. After the Taglang La, the passes, in order, are the Lachalung La (5,065 m/16,613 ft), the Nakli La (4,900 m/16,072 ft), the Bara Lacha La (4,880 m/16,006 ft) and the Rohtang La (3,990 m/13,087 ft).

Be prepared for bad weather on this route. The Indian state of Himachal Pradesh, into which you are riding, gets a very heavy monsoon and a certain amount of cloud invariably sneaks over the mountains

DESCRIPTION: A road tour – mostly rough tarmac and unmetalled jeep track – following the Indian National Highway 1B from Leh in Ladakh to Manali in Himachal Pradesh. Few mountain bike journeys are as challenging.

ROUTE LENGTH AND DURATION: 470 km (291 miles) (± 600 km/372 miles including acclimatization rides around Leh). 12–14 days biking (7–9 days *en route* and 3–5 days acclimatization).

WHEN TO GO: June–September. Snow is possible at higher elevations throughout the year.

SPECIAL CONSIDERATIONS: Mountain bike parts are unavailable anywhere in northern India. This route passes through largely uninhabited and extremely rugged country – lines of communication cannot be depended upon. Be prepared for extremes of climate and carry plenty of treated water as dehydration is a real issue here. Doing this trip unsupported will require legs like pistons and a very strong trailer or panniers. For an even more epic trip, consider riding the entire loop from Srinagar to Manali via Leh – allow a month! High-spec mountain bike recommended, plus support vehicle(s) and camping equipment.

MAPS: Leomann (Indian Himalaya) Maps –sheets three and five, 1:200,000.

TOUR OPERATORS: Very few foreign agencies offer trips this adventurous. KE Adventure Travel (www.keadventure.com) in the UK are a good first choice. In India contact Mandip Singh Soin at Ibex Expeditions (www.ibexexpeditions.com) or Out There Biking (www.out-there-biking.com).

PERMITS/RESTRICTIONS: None.

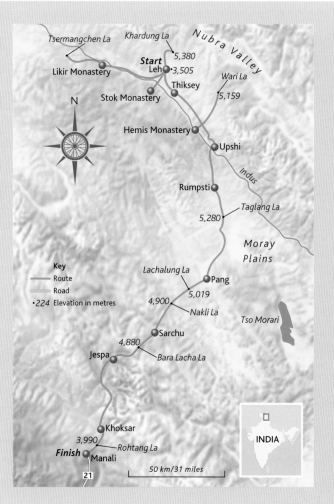

Tsermangchen La
Khardung La
Nubra Valley
Likir Monastery
Start
Leh · 5,380
· 3,505
Wari La
Thiksey
· 5,159
N
Stok Monastery
Hemis Monastery
Upshi
Indus
Rumpsti
Taglang La
5,280 ·
Moray Plains
Key
Lachalung La
Pang
Route
5,019
Road
4,900 ·
· 224 Elevation in metres
Nakli La
Tso Morari
Sarchu
4,880
Jespa
Bara Lacha La
Khoksar
3,990
Rohtang La
Finish Manali
21
50 km/31 miles
INDIA

to water the arid desert landscape of Ladakh. When it rains it absolutely pours, and the road is frequently washed out or blocked. Few complete this journey without their own tales of epic days and unforeseen circumstances. The biking is superlative though, and the gruelling climbs are rewarded with stupendous views and exhilarating descents. Few will forget having ridden the infamous Gata Loops on the descent from the Nakli La into the sensational valley of the Tsarap Lingti Chhu – a series of 22 hairpin bends that snake down a steep mountainside, with footpath shortcuts straight down available for those who really do like to fly. Ride carefully though – a new wheel rim or set of forks is a very long way away!

With every kilometre covered southwards the air becomes more humid, and riding up the final climb to the Rohtang you can often see the cloud pouring over the ridge from the other side. After days in the desiccated moonscape of Ladakh, the contrast as you sweep down from this pass into the lush forests and fragrant valleys of Himachal could hardly be more pronounced. You can practically drink the air, it is so moist.

The quality of this final descent can perhaps be assessed by the fact that my companions and I, having ridden it the previous day, hired jeeps and went back up for another blast. It is 52 km (32 miles) and over 2,000 m (6,560 ft) down from the top to Manali, where a comfortable hotel, hot shower and chilled Kingfisher beer await you.

◁ *A purely Tibetan landscape – crossing the Moray Plains, south of the Taglang La.*

▽ *In the valley of the Tsarap Lingti Chhu, south of the Lachalung/Nakli La crossing.*

TIBET
Lhasa to Kathmandu

STEVE RAZZETTI

▽ *On the first day's ride from Lhasa to the base of the Khamba La.*

King Songtsan Gampo founded the long forbidden and fabulously exotic city of Lhasa in the 7th century, and as an icon of the indomitable spirit of the Tibetan people and their colourful culture, the Potala Palace is perhaps only surpassed by the beaming countenance of its rightful resident, His Holiness the Dalai Lama. Situated in a comparatively sheltered basin at an altitude of 3,650 m (11,972 ft), Lhasa is one of the highest cities in the world and capital of what is today contentiously called the Tibet Autonomous Region by the Chinese.

△ *On the Khamba La.*

Kathmandu is probably even older. Though inhabited since at least 100 BC, the capital city of Nepal as we know it today was founded in AD 723. It is a place of startling paradoxes and contradictions, human and architectural, that mostly derive from unregulated and ballistic economic growth superimposed on an infrastructure that remains largely medieval. The Kathmandu Valley floor lies at 1,370 m (4,494 ft) above sea level, and the distinctive Newari pagoda-roofed temples of the city often seem to rise out of the ever-increasing traffic smog like fantastic apparitions. The snow-covered Himalayan summits that seem to loom right over the city in old photographs are today only visible from the teeming streets in instances of rare atmospheric clarity. The city was the epitome of hippy hedonism in the 1960s, and remains a popular destination for tourists, pilgrims and mountain adventurers of all persuasions.

Tibet has never been an easy place to get to. Francis Younghusband had to invade the country in 1904, and even then the authorities in Lhasa kept him waiting for days before they could decide whether or how to receive him. Today, one may arrive at the holy city by train, plane or automobile, but it is still an utterly outlandish place. The Friendship or Arniko Highway between Lhasa and Kathmandu was built by the Chinese in the 1960s, much to the consternation of the Indians who had lost a bloody border war with their northern neighbours in 1962.

▷ *Rongbuk monastery and the north face of Everest.*

▽ *Tandem maintenance at Gyantse.*

▽ OVERLEAF *Shyam Shah on the Pang La with the north face of Everest beyond.*

Although the dust, corrugations and rutted dirt that long made up the surface of this 'highway' are slowly but inexorably being smothered in tarmac as the Chinese modernize the region, the 1,000 km (620 mile) ride from Lhasa to Kathmandu remains the supreme biking challenge. Acclimatization to the altitude of Lhasa itself should ideally be given three or four days to occur before setting off, and both rider and bike must be thoroughly prepared for the six high passes *en route* and their associated gruelling climbs and exhilarating descents. There are no repair facilities, and no oases of luxury to retire to if the going gets too hard. This is not a trip for the faint-hearted.

Few will contemplate making this journey without the almost mandatory diversion to the north face base camp of Mount Everest at Rongbuk, and this will add three or four days and two further passes to an already challenging route. As the surfaced road becomes more prevalent and traffic increases, those with fat tyres and adventurous spirits will seek out other diversions and byways to vary their rides. One unmissable example is to start out by taking the old road between Lhasa and Shigatse, and travel via the Khamba La (4,794 m/15,724 ft), Nakartse, the Karo La (4,960 m/16,269 ft) and Gyantse. Views of the distant peaks on the border with Bhutan across the turquoise waters of Yamdrok Tso, and a visit to the Pelkhor Chorten or Kumbum at Gyantse, are but two reasons to make this diversion. Others include empty roads and preparing legs and lungs for their coming exertions.

From Shigatse, where time out to visit the vast monastic complex and seat of the Panchen Lama at Tashilunpo is obligatory, the road continues its westward sweep along the flanks of the Himalaya, with the passes getting higher and the road rougher as it heads toward Tingri. The diversion to Everest base camp and the Rongbuk Valley is made from here. Most go in and come out over the sensational Pang La (5,150 m/16,892 ft), from the crest of which a Himalayan panorama of jaw-dropping splendour is revealed. A more varied and challenging alternative is to go in via the Pang La and make a circuit via Rongbuk and the less travelled and rougher road out over the Lamma La (5,000 m/ 16,400 ft). There is a squalid but incredibly rejuvenating hot spring bath for those who can spare the time to go searching for it, just outside of Tingri itself. It's just about the only opportunity most riders will take for proper ablution during the entire route; Tibet is just too cold and windy!

Upon leaving Lhasa, this route never drops below 4,000 m (13,120 ft) in altitude again until the final descent into Nepal. The Gyamtso La (5,220 m/17,122 ft), between Shigatse and Tingri is the highest point on the route, but the final crossing of the Thang La (5,132 m/ 16,833 ft) will provide the images that just refuse to fade from memory. From its wide, windswept double crest the Himalaya seem close enough to reach out and touch, and the views to Shishapangma – the only 8,000 m (26,240 ft) peak entirely within Tibet – are simply sensational.

It is the descent from this pass that has entered biking folklore, however. No superlatives can come remotely close to evoking the thrill of setting off from this pass, knowing that it is all downhill to the border and beyond. Down to the sweltering, plant-scented, insect-screaming valley of the Bhote Khosi. Down for two whole days. Down 4,600 m (15,088 ft) over 120 km (74 miles) of switchbacks, off-road shortcuts, hell-for-leather straights and insanely dangerous wash-outs. My Nepali companion proudly unclipped his speedometer at the bottom and thrust it under my nose. Maximum speed – 97 kph (60 mph). Flying! The final 1,400 m (4,592 ft) climb to Dhulikel on the Kathmandu valley rim is long enough, but by then your altitude-acclimatized lungs will be delivering so much oxygen to your leg muscles that you'll barely notice it.

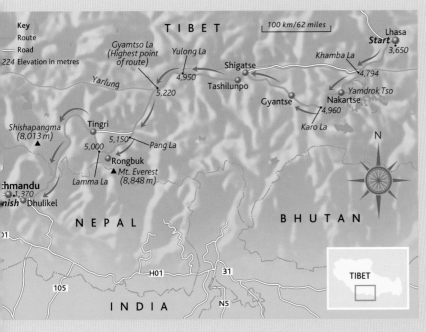

facts and figures

DESCRIPTION: An epic high altitude journey from the Tibetan plateau to the capital of Nepal.

ROUTE LENGTH AND DURATION: ± 1,000 km (620 miles), 17–20 days of strenuous riding.

WHEN TO GO: June–August

SPECIAL CONSIDERATIONS: Take a mid- to high-spec mountain bike(fully serviced) and a decent spares kit. Without support vehicle(s) and tents this trip is truly hardcore. Continuous high altitude and extremely harsh climate should be prepared for. If you contemplate doing this unsupported or independently, be aware that riding a fully laden bike on these roads can define torture!

TOUR OPERATORS: From the UK, KE Adventure Travel (www.keadventure.com). From Nepal, Himalaya Expeditions (www.himexnepal.com).

PERMITS/RESTRICTIONS: It is possible to do this trip independently, but the Chinese authorities will not make things easy for you.

NEPAL
Pokhara to Kathmandu

STEVE RAZZETTI

Nepal has made a special place for itself in the hearts of all who have travelled there. There is an ineffable exoticism to the place. "The wildest dreams of Kew are the facts of Kathmandu" wrote Rudyard Kipling, and few first-time visitors can fail to feel their pulse quicken at the sight of the city's pagoda-roofed temples and enormous Buddhist *stupas* rising above the maelstrom of rickshaws, pedestrians, weaving motorbikes, laden porters and buses way too large for the narrow streets. This frisson does not fade!

There seem to be temples everywhere in the capital. Ochre-daubed *saddhus* sit, lotus-legged, giving *tikkhas* to the faithful as bells clang and the powerful scent of incense fills the air. Pious Buddhist pilgrims chant for alms, their prayer wheels constantly turning, while

▽ *Riders on one of several excellent day excursions from Pokhara – the 55 km (34 mile) Sarangkot circuit.*

above them the iconic eyes of the Buddha stare out in all four directions over the city and the valley beyond. The country became famous in the 1960s as a Mecca for hippies, with all manner of people descending on the place in search of one form of enlightenment or another. Bill Tilman was a member of the first group of Westerners ever permitted to explore the country outside the Kathmandu Valley in 1948, and he wryly observed that "Wise men traditionally come from the East, and it is probable that to them the West and its ways were suspect long before we ourselves began to have doubts."

The history of Nepal has been chequered of late. For a decade between 1996 and 2006 the tourism industry upon which the country so heavily depends hung on in the face of a Maoist insurgency that verged on civil war. This ended with a ceasefire in 2006, and on 28 May 2008, Constitutional Assembly elections were finally held in which the Maoists participated. On 29 May the newly elected assembly voted by a massive 560 to 4 to abolish the monarchy and declare a Federal Republic, and on 11 June the hugely unpopular King Gyanendra left his palace, bringing to an end a dynasty that had ruled the country since Prithvi Narayan Shah first unified it in 1768.

It was mountaineers and scientists that really opened the eyes of the wider world to the peerless realm of the Nepal Himalaya, making Everest and the sherpas living in its shadow into household names the world over. Twelve years after Edmund Hillary and

▽ *Annapurna Himal at dawn from Begnas Tal.*

Sherpa Tenzing returned from the summit of Everest having made the first ascent on 29 May 1953, Jimmy Roberts founded Mountain Travel Nepal and started what was to become Nepal's most lucrative industry – trekking. Western preoccupations with celebrity and superlative have meant that the areas around the biggest peaks have seen the most of both the benefits and the side-effects of this booming trade, while the rest of the country remains relatively unknown.

Getting off the beaten track, even by a few hundred metres, still takes you into a country largely unaffected by the whirlwind of 21st century development, and no method of travel is as suited to exploring the middle-hills and villages as perfectly as mountain biking. This journey

DESCRIPTION: A back-country off-road trip from Pokhara to Kathmandu in Nepal.

ROUTE LENGTH AND DURATION: 350 km (217 miles), 10 days riding.

WHEN TO GO: March–April or October–December.

SPECIAL CONSIDERATIONS: Mid-spec mountain bike required. Be aware that baggage limits on internal flights in Nepal will preclude flying to Pokhara with your bike.

MAPS: Nepal 1:500,000, Reise Verlag, Nepal 1:750,000, GeoCentre.

TOUR OPERATORS: KE Adventure Travel (www.keadventure. com) and Dawn til Dusk (www.nepalbiking.com).

PERMITS/RESTRICTIONS: None.

ACCOMMODATION: Hotels in Pokhara, Gorkha and Kathmandu – otherwise camping.

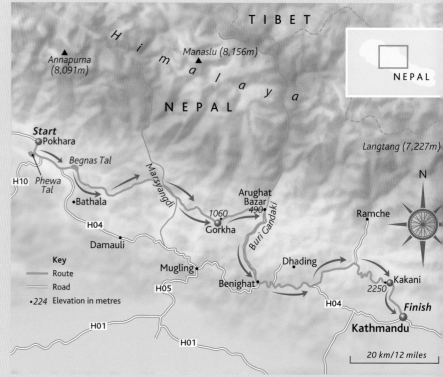

is an illustration in point. The country between Kathmandu and Pokhara is seen by most visitors today either from the window of a plane or a bus, and the real charms of Gorkha and the lower Marsyangdi and Trisuli rivers thus elude them.

Arise before dawn in Pokhara and you will be treated to sunrise on one of the Himalaya's most iconic vistas – that of Machhapuchhare and the Annapurnas reflected in the tranquil waters of Phewa Tal. Ride your mountain bike up onto the Kali Horseshoe and the view is even better. Descend to Begnas Tal and spend the next night there for an equally magical sunrise the next day, but one that very few others will have seen.

Three days of fantastic singletrack and unused jeep road through sleepy backwater villages then bring you to the elevated town of Gorkha, where you will find it difficult to resist a cool beer on the terrace as the sun sinks over the foothills into the Indian plains. This is the halfway point of the trip, and a pause here is well rewarded. The medieval *durbar* ('palace') of Prithvi Narayan Shah is a short walk up the ridge above the centre of town, and there are numerous possibilities for day rides also.

Perhaps the climax of this ride is saved for the last though, with a lung-busting 1,600 m (5,248 ft) climb on a quiet road out of the Trisuli Valley and up onto the Kathmandu Valley rim at Kakani. Given clear skies, the sunrise panorama from this spot is breathtaking, with the mighty peaks of the Nepal Himalaya, from Annapurna in the west to Gauri Shankar in the east, lined up along the northern skyline. All that then remains between you and a slap-up meal in a Kathmandu restaurant is a ballistic final downhill through the Nagarjun Forest Reserve.

△ *A camp at Kakani on the Kathmandu Valley rim, with the Langtang and Annapurna Himal beyond.*

◁ FAR LEFT *Crossing the Buri Gandakhi on a wire bridge.*

▽ OVERLEAF *The descent from Kakani to Kathmandu through the Nagarjun Forest Reserve.*

BHUTAN
West to East

STEVE RAZZETTI

In 1616 from Tibet, there arrived in Druk Yul ('the Land of the Drukpas') a religious leader by the name of Ngawang Namgyel. Fleeing persecution and fearing for his life, he came to the southern valleys seeking refuge from those Tibetans who disputed his recognition as the incarnation of Pema Karpo, a famous Drukpa scholar. He must have been quite a character, as within 30 years he had unified the area and established dominion over the territory that we know today as Bhutan.

In Bhutanese history he is known as *Shabdrung*, and his legacy is indeed great. He built many of the spectacular *dzongs* or fortified monasteries that characterize the Bhutanese landscape to this day, and instigated a system of government that separated the state clergy under a chief abbot or *Je Khenpo* from the theocracy under a secular leader or *Desi*. This until the establishment of the monarchy in 1907.

The Bhutanese royal family took an enlightened approach to the government of the country, famously claiming to aspire to raising the Gross National Happiness rather than the Gross National Product. Only in 1999 was the first TV station inaugurated and internet access permitted within the kingdom, and in 2005 the revered king, Jigme Singye Wangchuk, stunned the nation by announcing his imminent abdication as absolute monarch in favour of a parliamentary democracy.

Just two years after ascending the throne, Jigme Singye Wangchuk opened Bhutan's doors to tourism for the first time in 1974, with the avowed intention of pursuing a 'high value, low volume' approach. That year just 287 people visited the country – a figure that rose to almost 3,000

▽ *Dancing monks at the annual* tsechu *(festival) at Tashichleodzong in the capital, Thimpu.*

in 1992 and is nearer 8,000 today, netting the country in excess of $9 million in foreign exchange. Until 1991, the Bhutan Tourism Corporation ran everything, and foreign tourists were only permitted to come as their 'guests'. Subsequently the industry has been privatized, and there are over 200 licensed operators in Bhutan today.

Modern Bhutan is a country of some 47,000 square kilometres (18,330 square miles – roughly the size of Switzerland) with a population of a little over 650,000. It is bordered to the north by Tibet, to the south by the Indian states of Assam and West Bengal, to the east by the Indian state of Arunachal Pradesh and in the west by Sikkim. On its border with Tibet lies the highest unclimbed peak in the world, Gangkar Puensum.

Perhaps uniquely in the 21st century, Bhutan has striven successfully to preserve its traditional culture and way of life, the authenticity of its religious festivals, its vernacular architecture and monuments and its pristine natural environment – 65 per cent of the country is still forested. All of these qualities make it somewhat special in our globalized, materialist world, and most visitors alighting from their flights at Paro still share the same sentiments expressed by the Earl of Ronaldshay, who described his arrival in Bhutan in 1921 thus: "With our passage through the bridge, behold a curious transformation. For just as Alice, when she walked through the looking-glass, found herself in a new and whimsical

▽ *On the Dochu La between Thimpu and Punakha.*

DESCRIPTION: A road tour – mostly rough tarmac – west to east across Bhutan.

ROUTE LENGTH AND DURATION: 880 km (546 miles), 9 or 10 days in the saddle.

WHEN TO GO: March–April or October–November.

SPECIAL CONSIDERATIONS: High-spec mountain bike or hybrid recommended, with slick or semi-slick tyres. Bhutan is not cheap – currently travel within the country costs $200 per person per day, and this is due to increase to $250. Baggage allowances on Druk Air into Paro are only 20 kg (44 lbs) per ticket, so if you are bringing your bike, pack very sparingly or be prepared to pay for excess.

TOUR OPERATORS: KE Adventure Travel (www.keadventure.com), Wilderness Journeys (www.wildernessjourneys.com) and Adventure Consultants (www.adventureconsultants.co.nz). In Bhutan, Keys to Bhutan (www.keystobhutan.com).

PERMITS/RESTRICTIONS: Independent travel is not possible in Bhutan – your arrangements will have to be made by a government-licensed travel company.

ACCOMMODATION: Hotel and hostel accommodation – of varying standard but mostly excellent – is available throughout this route. If you need to camp, your agent will provide all the necessary food and equipment.

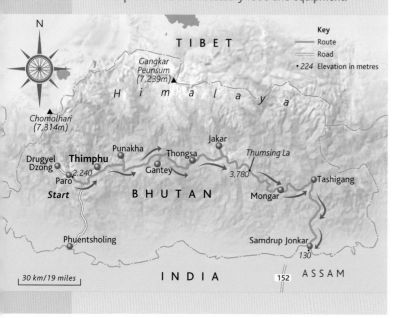

world, so we, when we crossed the Pa-Chhu, found ourselves, as though caught up in some magic time machine fitted fantastically with a reverse, flung back across the centuries into the feudalism of a medieval age." It is a very special place.

There is really only one road in the country – the west–east highway or Lateral Road, from Phuentsholing in the west to Trashigang in the east – and it is upon this that this route is based. Traffic throughout the kingdom is never more than light and the one traffic light for which the capital – Thimpu – was famed has recently been removed.

Construction of the west–east highway was started in 1962 and took over 15 years to complete. It was only

built to a standard width of 2.5 m (8.2 ft), and though surfaced for most of its length the tarmac is of poor quality. The western section is maintained by the DANTAK division of the Indian Border Roads Organization, the rest by the Bhutanese Department of Roads. Japanese aid is financing the replacement of some of the more dodgy bridges, but overall the road still presents a formidable challenge to bikers.

Available transport connections will mean that for most, this is a ride from the airport at Paro in the west, across the country to Tashigang and then out south into Assam at Samdrup Jonkar. There is very little flat country *en route*, and by the time you reach the sweltering heat at the Indian border (altitude a mere 130 m/426 ft) you will have clocked up a mind-boggling 15,800 m (51,824 ft) of ascent and 18,200 m (59,696 ft) of descent. The climbs are very long and the descents over too quickly, but resist the urge to treat this as a road race and take your time to enjoy the enchanting country you are passing through. Punakha, Gantey and Thongsa especially are magical places, steeped in history and well worth pausing to explore.

△ *At the Pele La.*

◁ ABOVE LEFT *A monk with a mountain bike.*

JAPAN
The Inland Sea and Aso Caldera

CAROLE EDRICH

The ancient country of Japan offers myriad cultural and historical traditions, picture-perfect vistas and an extensive network of well-paved backroads and alternative routes. Two-wheeled travel is popular here and friendly locals welcome foreign cyclists with a warmth and consideration rarely seen elsewhere. While traversing a diverse yet representative portion of this exotic land, this route affords travellers an opportunity to experience the country's age-old traditions, visit ancient temples, rugged coastlines and serene hot springs and sample some staggeringly mouthwatering food.

▽ *A shinto priest on a bike in Kyoto.*

The altitude of the first two days is relatively constant, rising from Kyoto through Arashiyama to the densely wooded hills of Miyajima. Crossing the island of Honshu, the trail descends to Higashiyama village, before winding upwards to the Gonami Pass at 850 m (2,788 ft) and descending into Natasho Valley and the coastal fishing town of Obama. The lowest part of the Five Lakes section is Mikata at 19 m (62 ft) and the highest Wakasa at 357 m (1,171 ft), after which the ferry is taken to Beppu on Kyushu Island. Next follows a climb to Mount Kuju pass (1,500 m/4,920 ft) on the way to the world's largest caldera. It traverses the edge of an active volcanic crater, rolling green pastures and smoke-belching mountains and descends to 299 m (981 ft), finally crossing the low Chojabara Plateau and dirt tracks of Mount Kuju's foothills on the way back to Yufuin.

In Kyoto the route winds through narrow streets showing a microcosm of modern high-tech and ancient traditional culture so typical of today's urban Japan. Gion District, the ancient entertainment and geisha centre, is comprised of tiny streets, ancient temples and modern prefab buildings, and even today it's possible to catch a glimpse of a geisha or *maiko* (trainee geisha) as they go about their business. Further east, Kiyomizu Dera has more traditional Japanese quarters and a huge temple that provides an expansively attractive view of the town.

In densely wooded hills suffused with the smell of the spectacular cedar trees, it's occasionally possible to spot the wild boar, bears and monkeys that make the area their home.

△ *The Umeda Sky Building in Osaka.*

DESCRIPTION: A wide-ranging tour through a large part of Japan.

ROUTE LENGTH AND DURATION: 700 km (434 miles) exclusive of ferry/train rides, 11 days (3–4 days of optional extra diversions).

WHEN TO GO: Year-round, although April–May and September–October are best. Autumn is a stunning show, when mountains and gardens assume the colours of fire in a carpet of reds, burnished coppers and bright yellows. In spring the city fills with soft pink and white snow-like petals.

SPECIAL CONSIDERATIONS: Hybrid/mountain bike required. Take clothing suitable for warm valleys and damp, cold mountains – you'll pass through both. Regular clothes or coverings are required for temple visits, and take something suitable for hot baths.

MAPS: Footprint Japan.

TOUR OPERATORS: Saddle Skedaddle.

PERMITS/RESTRICTIONS: None.

ACCOMMODATION: Suisen-Kyo, Miyama Youth Hostel, Hotel Obama, Kikugawa, Momiji-so, Mikata-no Ryokan Onsen, Biwa-ko-no Ryokan, Sensui Minshuku Onsen, Akamizu Lodge and Makiba-no-ie are all recommended.

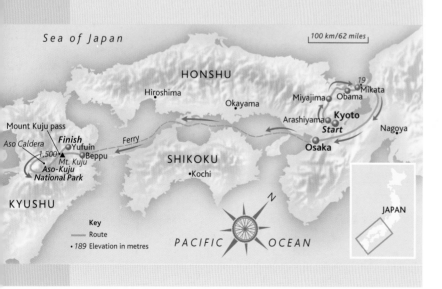

The well-surfaced roads traverse low mountain passes and small rice paddy valleys dotted with typical old Japanese farmhouses. Miyama is a treasure of an island, with huge red shrines rising out of the water and temples made of camphor wood. Guarding the Itsukushima shrine, this is the largest *torii* ('gate') of its kind.

Some of the following roads have been used by traders for thousands of years, and the winding climb to Gonami pass is rewarded by a long and beautiful descent. With rugged coastlines and tiny fishing hamlets, the Omaba area is home to several Soto Zen temples, the largest of which nestles amongst centuries-old cedar trees. Biwa-ko, the largest freshwater lake in Japan, is home to over 60 varieties of fish, many of which have an exquisite flavour. The

roads, which are both paved and unpaved, weave through dense, verdant valleys. Picturesque villages alternate with marshlands, grassy beaches and tree-lined shores, and both dawn and dusk offer breathtaking photo opportunities.

After transferring to Osaka by train and ferry to Kyushu Island, the route traverses Beppu. This area boasts the highest number of thermal sources and gush volume in Japan. Steam rises from thousands of hot spring vents, while the imposing Tsurumi Mountain is a constant backdrop. The route gradually ascends through the Aso-Kuju National Park to Mount Kuju Pass and a stunning downhill ride that sweeps through a landscape of dark, extinct volcanoes, verdant open meadows and profusely vegetated forests. This breathtakingly steep descent gradually reveals the sheer size and scale of the Aso Caldera.

Many take extra time to explore the numerous off-road trails and roads that criss-cross this caldera. Paths follow the soft curves of four of its central cones as well as the rougher fifth, which is still active. The route then meanders easily through remote grassy slopes below the smoking crater above, then takes a combination of narrow tarmac roads and mountain dirt tracks, passing a stunningly high suspension bridge and its view of two waterfalls cascading down to the deep valley floor, before returning to the Onsen town of Yufuin and the journey's end.

△ *The spectacular Aso Caldera.*

◁ FAR LEFT *A detail on Nijo Castle in Kyoto.*

AUSTRALASIA

"Ambition leads me not only farther than any other man has been before me, but as far as I think it possible for man to go."

JAMES COOK

△ *Cycling past termite mounds in Lakefield National Park.*

The landing of Captain James Cook at Botany Bay on 29 April 1770 is something most of us learn about at school, but the enormity of the man's achievements still escapes most of us. He was at sea – firstly aboard *Endeavour*, and then *Resolution* – almost continuously for over 11 years from 1768–79, in the process becoming the first man to circumnavigate the globe. He then repeated the feat in the other direction and visited both the Arctic and Antarctic. Singlehandedly he unravelled the geography of the Pacific Ocean, revealing in the process the true extents of New Zealand and Australia.

The continent that Captain Cook so boldly claimed for England is a place like nowhere on earth. Covering an area of 7.6 million square kilometres (2.96 million square miles) with a coastline of over 34,200 km (21,204 miles), the vast majority of Australia is arid, sun-scorched desert, or outback. Few that have travelled across it will forget the sheer scale and flatness of the landscape, the searing heat or the intense red colour of the earth. This creates a fine,

all-permeating dust, traces of which will linger in hidden corners of vehicles, clothing
and bikes for years. Not for nothing is the middle of Australia known as the Red Centre.

It is along the coast of Australia, where the climate is affected by the oceans, that the
greatest variations in natural environments are found. The southeast and southwest corners
are temperate zones, while in the north the climate is tropical, with rainforests, grasslands and
mangrove swamps. The oceans surrounding Australia themselves support an incredible array of
flora and fauna, with the Great Barrier Reef alone supporting 1,500 species of fish and 30
species of whale and dolphin.

Outdoor pursuits of all kinds are hugely popular in Australia – Barry Humphries quipped
that "Australia is an outdoor country. People only go inside to use the toilet and that's only a
recent development." Cycling at all levels is a big part of this outdoor life, and long-distance
routes are being pioneered countrywide. The longest is the Bicentennial, which stretches for
5,330 km (3,305 miles) up the east coast from Healesville, Victoria, to Cooktown in Queensland.

2,217 km (1,375 miles) southeast of Sydney across the Tasman Sea lies Wellington, New
Zealand. James Cook sailed around both the South and North Islands of New Zealand on his
way to Botany Bay, but he was not the first European to see Aotearoa, as the Maoris call it –
'the Land of the Long White Cloud'. That distinction belonged to Abel Tasman, the Dutch
master navigator, 128 years previously in 1642. The population of New Zealand today is
approximately 4.2 million, of whom all but a million live on the smaller North Island. Maori
language and culture is Polynesian, as the first settlers came from Samoa and Tonga (Hawaiki)
a thousand years ago. The climate is maritime, varying from subtropical at the top of the
North Island to cool temperate on the west coast of the South Island, and few places on
earth feel, or indeed are, so far from everywhere else.

There is so much that is truly unique about New Zealand. The stupendous mountains
and lakes of the South Island may feel familiar to alpinists, but where can compare to Milford
Sound? Where is there a landscape like the Tongariro National Park and Ruapehu on the North
Island? The central plateau is a mysterious land of geysers, bubbling mud pools and active
volcanoes. Ruapehu itself erupted in spectacular fashion as recently as 1995–96, forcing the
closure of both ski resorts and airports. 80 per cent of New Zealand flora is endemic, and apart
from bats there were no mammals whatsoever for several million years until the arrival of
man. Bird life in New Zealand made up for this lack of mammals with an incredibly diverse and
specialized range of species. Sitting in the woods at dawn or dusk, listening to an other-wordly
and completely enchanting chorus of tuis, kakas, rurus and korimakos is as unforgettable as
the sound of the world's only Alpine parrot – the fearless kea – attempting to remove the
windscreen-wiper blades from your campervan or break into your tent as you cower inside.

△ A team effort through a
difficult creek crossing on
the Old Telegraph Track.

AUSTRALIA
Cape York

ANDREW BAIN

▽ *Riding past a crocodile warning notice in Lakefield National Park.*

Australia is a land filled with epic road journeys, be it the unwavering and unchanging Nullarbor Plain, the desert distances of the Stuart Highway between Adelaide and Darwin, or the *Mad Max* landscapes of outback New South Wales. For most Australians, however, the ultimate road adventure is Cape York, the country's northernmost point. From Cairns, the nearest large town, it's a 1,200 km (744 mile) journey along some of the most difficult roads in the country, travelling through bulldust, corrugations, sand, heat, river crossings and the threat of crocodiles. Against this, even the Nullarbor can seem like little more than a lengthy commute. Most people who travel to Cape York do so in 4x4 vehicles, but a few come by bike, discovering the outback at both its most beautiful and brutal. Distances can be massive – from Cooktown through Lakefield National Park it's 270 km (167 miles) just to the next roadhouse – and logistics complicated, but the rewards are just as large.

In such tough country the temptation is to take the direct route to the tip, following the heavily corrugated Peninsula Development Road, which is at times so straight it might have been designed by a city planner. But there's so much beauty on the peninsula, and so little of it is visible from the main drag. Instead, there is a series of less-travelled tracks – the Bloomfield Track, Lakefield National Park and the Old Telegraph Track – that bypass large sections of the Development Road. They might take cyclists away from the trickle of services along the peninsula, but when you're encased inside the Daintree rainforest, cooling down beneath isolated Eliot Falls, or watching jabirus take flight from the roadside, the condition of the roads can easily be forgiven.

Each of the tracks has its unique cycling difficulties and pleasures. The controversial Bloomfield Track begins at the holiday town of Cape Tribulation and carves through the northern edges of the World Heritage-listed Daintree rainforest. Constructed in the face of environmental protest in the 1980s, its builders clearly decided to minimize damage to the forest by doing without switchbacks and bends through the mountains, resulting in gradients of up to 33 per cent through the Cowie and Donovan Ranges.

Beyond Cooktown, a second side track heads through Lakefield National Park, where termite mounds rise like gravestones and a plethora of birdlife wanders the swamps. Hard-packed and traffic-free much of the time, this road can seem like a ready-made bike path, but it has a downside – Lakefield is one of Australia's major estuarine crocodile breeding areas. Camped one night beside the Laura River during our ride to the tip, we had a visit from a crocodile, making our tents seem more like lunch bags.

At Musgrave Roadhouse, riders have no choice but to follow the Development Road for a few days – a half-time break of sorts between the pleasures of Cape York Peninsula – before turning onto the Old Telegraph Track at Bramwell Roadhouse. Once the main route to Cape York, the unmaintained track has more sand than most beaches, and it can take an hour to ride the first 6 km (4 miles). Eroded to the point that it's impassable to most 4x4s, it is also the Cape's most spectacular stretch of road, switching between thick forest and flowering heathlands and laced with cooling creeks and waterfalls.

▽ *Hauling a bike across Cockatoo Creek on the Old Telegraph Track.*

DESCRIPTION: Rugged bush tracks to Australia's northern tip.

ROUTE LENGTH AND DURATION: 1,200 km (744 miles); allow 2–3 weeks.

WHEN TO GO: Cape York's tracks are passable only in winter; the wet season runs from around November to March.

SPECIAL CONSIDERATIONS: Mountain bikes, tents, camp stoves and fuel all required. Cape York is brutal on bikes and parts are difficult to source, so carry plenty of spares. You'll need to carry up to five days of food at a time or mail food drops to stations ahead of your departure.

MAPS: Hema's Cape York map is the most detailed and useful.

TOUR OPERATORS: There are no special cycle tours to Cape York.

PERMITS/RESTRICTIONS: None.

ACCOMMODATION: There is accommodation at some roadhouses, towns and stations, but you will need to camp most of the time.

After all this, cyclists arrive at Cape York to discover one final, cruel fact – the road ends 400 m (1,312 ft) short of the tip, at the base of the headland that peters away to become Australia's northern finish. We tried mountain biking to its end but the rock defeated us. Instead, we shouldered the bikes and walked them to the ocean's edge, parking them against the small sign that announced, 'You are standing at the northernmost point of the Australian continent.'

Here, it has become travelling tradition to pop open a bottle of champagne to celebrate the achievement of reaching Australia's apex. Cyclists will have earned the bubbly more than anyone, but who wants to carry the bottle on these roads?

△ *A cyclist overlooking Frangipani Beach from the headland at the tip of Cape York.*

◁ *Pushing through a sandy track in Lakefield National Park.*

▽ OVERLEAF *Riding across the Dulhunty River on the Old Telegraph Track.*

DESCRIPTION: Rail trail (mixed hard-packed gravel/pebble surface) across scenic, remote southeast New Zealand.

ROUTE LENGTH AND DURATION: 150 km (93 miles), 3–4 days.

WHEN TO GO: All year, but winter can be very cold.

SPECIAL CONSIDERATIONS: Take toilet paper (none in toilets), bike lights (for tunnels), basic bike tools, sunblock, rain gear and water (not readily available outside towns).

MAPS: Download from www.otagocentralrailtrail.co.nz.

TOUR OPERATORS: See www.otagocentralrailtrail.co.nz.

PERMITS/RESTRICTIONS: All guided groups need a concession from the Department of Conservation.

ACCOMMODATION: Campsites, hostels and guest houses aplenty. In summer book in advance; otherwise, you should have no problem just turning up and they'll find you somewhere, although less places are open in winter.

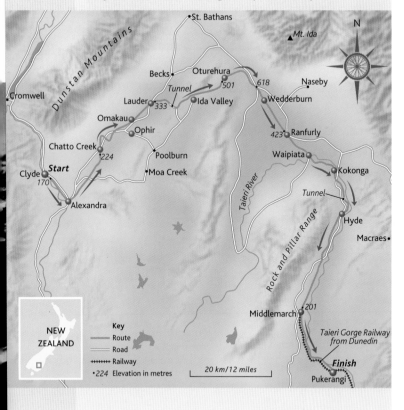

The trail itself is not exactly mountainous. True, it climbs from 170 m (558 ft) at Clyde to 618 m (2,027 ft) near Wedderburn, but it's all rail trail-flat or gently sloping. You will need a mountain bike, however, or one as sturdy as. The surface is a mix of hard-packed gravel and crunchy pebbles. Though better than it used to be when it opened in 2000, there are still a few bumpy stretches. The route roughly traces three sides of a square, so be prepared for both headwinds and tailwinds at some points.

You might be tempted to hurtle along the 150 km (93 mile) trail in one long single summer's day (when it doesn't get dark until 10pm), but the operators strongly discourage anyone, even the very fit, from attempting it. This is a trip to take at leisure: rural New Zealand doesn't rush things. Take three or four days, chat to locals, take up your hostel or guest house's offer of a free day's canoe loan or horse ride, enjoy a robust chat about rugby or cricket with a farmer over a village-bar beer. Savour the breezy isolation of your gentle momentum between settlements; just you, your bike, and the hills.

The trail starts at Clyde and finishes at Middlemarch – but carry on 21 km (13 miles) beyond that, along deserted dirt roads amid more stunning scenery, to Pukerangi. Here, at a tiny station so remote it seems to have been left there by accident, you can catch a daily service along the jaw-dropping Taieri Gorge to Dunedin on a 1920s train of wood, tin and improbably ancient colours. Heard great things about the Christchurch to Greymouth railway? Well, this is better. It drops you off in Dunedin, 'Edinburgh of the South'. It will feel more like New York after your few days of psychological detox at Kiwi-country pace.

▷ *A cyclist approaches Poolburn Gorge Tunnel.*

NORTH AMERICA

"The grand show is eternal. It is always sunrise somewhere; the dew is never dried all at once; a shower is forever falling; vapour is ever rising. Eternal sunrise, eternal dawn and gloaming, on sea and continents and islands, each in its turn, as the round earth rolls."

JOHN MUIR

△ *The White Rim Trail unfolds along the arid buttes and mesas of Canyonlands National Park, Utah.*

The frontier has always been central to the American sense of identity. The notion of an untamed wilderness beyond remains key to understanding the way Americans relate to their great outdoors. It is one of the world's great paradoxes that the country with the highest levels of vehicle use, energy consumption and *per capita* carbon emissions, is today home to a people for whom the stewardship and protection of the wild and untrammelled places in their domain is paramount. It was in California that the first state park was founded in Yosemite in 1864, and in Wyoming that the world's first national park was established at Yellowstone. The US National Park Service was created in 1916 and is today responsible for 58 national parks and hundreds of other national monuments and historic buildings. Practically all of America's iconic landscapes are within its protective embrace – the Grand Canyon, Washington's North Cascades, Utah's Arches and Zion, Alaska's Glacier Bay... Parks Canada was not far behind, with Banff National Park in the Canadian Rockies founded in 1885.

Americans certainly like to get 'out there'. America's National Park Service and Parks Canada have excellent web resources (www.nps.gov and www.pc.gc.ca) and an ethos of conservation and public service that puts many others to shame. This is largely due to the boundless enthusiasm and dedication of men such as John Muir. Originally from Scotland, Muir's family emigrated to Wisconsin in 1849 when he was just 11 years old. His legendary association with Yosemite and boundless enthusiasm for the wilderness was instrumental in setting the whole US parks system in motion. In 1903 he took President Theodore Roosevelt wild camping in the back country of Yosemite, and during evening fireside conversations convinced him of the need for government control and management of such natural assets.

This feeling of stewardship and appreciation of the great natural heritage of the Americas has not been confined to backwoodsmen, mountaineers and hikers, however. In 1972 Greg Siple was riding his bike along the coast of California during an epic 29,000 km (17,980 mile) trip from Anchorage, Alaska to Tierra del Fuego. He had raised sponsorship from *National Geographic* for this, calling the venture Hemistour. An idea came to him as he pedalled along. Why not commemorate the impending American bicentennial with a ride across the country? Why not invite folk from all over to participate? Why not call it Bikecentennial?

From this seed germinated an organization of almost fanatically enthusiastic volunteers and friends, culminating in 1976 with a 6,843 km (4,250 mile) tour between Yorktown, Virginia, and Astoria, Oregon. Over 4,000 people participated, 2,000 of them completing the entire route. The legacy of this mammoth logistical effort continues today in the form of the Adventure Cycling Association, from whose offices in Missoula, Montana, are available route plans, expert advice and guidance, and organized tours on a network of bike trails that criss-cross the entire USA.

Americans like to compete with each other more than most, and some people just have to race. Criteriums – fixed time or lap races over short courses, usually in urban settings – may be the most popular form of bike racing in the US, but the hardcore go for the Race Across America, which makes even the Tour de France seem tame. John Marino came up with the idea in 1978, when he rode across the country in just 13 days. The first race was held in 1982 and won by Lon Haldeman. It has subsequently become something of a national occasion. Unlike the Tour, there are no stages and the clock ticks continuously from start to finish. Riders have to balance rest/sleep periods with time in the saddle, with many averaging 22 hours' riding a day. The course is a gruelling 4,830 km (3,000 miles) from Oceanside, California, to Annapolis in Maryland, but the exact route has varied, so records are set according to average speeds attained. In 1986 Pete Penseyres rode 5,000 km (3,100 miles) in 8 days, 9 hours and 47 minutes, averaging 15.4 mph (24.8 kph). It makes your calves twitch just thinking about it!

▽ *Heading south through the Devil's Slide area on California's Pacific Coast bicycle route.*

USA
Moab, Utah

JACQUES MARAIS

▷ *The White Rim Trail runs along the Green and Colorado River courses.*

▽ *You have to trust your tyres along Slickrock's sandstone drop-offs.*

Moab. Now there's a four letter word epitomizing everything that is über-cool about mountain biking. The name of this little town in Utah must have launched hundreds of biking brands, and it is surely the Arcadia every member of the fat-track tribe dreams about. This is where you will find the legendary Slickrock Trail, the truly hair-raising Poison Spider Loop, and horizon-to-horizon cranking along legendary multi-day routes such as the White Rim Canyon Trail. But there is life to Moab beyond Eddie McStiff burgers, Tyre Bite lagers and stomach-lurching drop-offs. Just the drive along the green, crushed-ice course of the mighty Colorado is enough to skid your endorphins into amber alert. Grand buttes, flat-topped mesas and rocky towers shatter the skyline beyond Castle Valley, while craggy fins rout the landscape below the distant La Sal peaks.

The name Moab itself is Biblical (after the country of the Moabites) and comes courtesy of the devout Mormons who originally settled this part of the Utah desert. Cruise onto the main drag, and you're bound to feel like a teenager on a first date as you ogle a riot of bike shops named after the famous trails blasting through the surrounding red rock ridges. Rim Cyclery, Poison Spider Bicycles, Slickrock Cycles... this has got to be living the mountain biking dream.

You can approach your Moab epiphany in a number of ways. Either opt for a crank along one of the multi-day trails (Kokopelli and White Rim Canyon are the obvious choices), or base yourself in town and do a range of gut-thumping, mouth-watering, tyre-shredding rides you're sure to remember for the rest of your life.

Day one is the Slickrock Trail. Arguably the world's most famous mountain bike trail, Slickrock is rated an undiluted, 100 per cent Black Route. In fact, the signs at the trailhead warn you explicitly to stay off the trail if you in any way doubt your technical skills. Getting to the trailhead itself is no big deal, and it won't take you more than 20 minutes to pedal up the steep Sand Flats Road zigzagging out of town. Once you reach the top, it's just you and miles of curvaceous sandstone. Knobs and spurs, fins and outcrops and gashed canyons

are frozen in time, as if the outdoor gods got together during the early Cretaceous period to shape the perfect mountain bike playground. The 3.2 km (2 mile) practice loop serves as a taster, but the real test kicks in once you crank onto the 16 km (10 mile) Slickrock Trail.

"You've gotta trust your rubber!" my friend Mike shouts as we set off, immediately dropping down 3 m (10 ft) along a steep rock chute. Momentum is the name of the game, and all you can do is focus as you blast along the dotted white line traversing the slalom sandstone slope. Looping whorls of entrada sandstone lure you ever onwards, enticing you to bomb improbable lines on the very edge of gaping canyons. High above, white clouds scud against the dome of the sky, cotton-wooling from the Colorado River far below you to the opposite horizon, where the snowy La Sal peaks spike against the blue. It is like riding within a multi-million dollar movie set, and three hours later you will finally tick off Slickrock on your 'Legendary Rides' list, sporting a smile big enough to swallow an MTB tyre.

On day two, if you're in search of a trail packing serious venom, head approximately 17 km (11 miles) northwest along the US-191 and US-279. You will find the start of the Poison Spider Trail on a dirt road (look out for a sign reading 'Dinosaur Tracks'). This menacing ride is rated as Double Black, and trail guides describe it as 'gruelling' and even 'life threatening'. The Portal section, with a 130 m (426 ft) drop edging the singletrack, has been responsible for serious injuries and at least one confirmed death, so take extra care.

The first mile or two is made up of vicious inclines, mashed together by baby-head rocks and stretches of calf-crunching sand. Then you hit The Ledges, and it's like riding up two steps at a time before you eventually crest onto the alluvial plain. From here, the views

▽ BELOW RIGHT *February snow dusts Slickrock's amber sandstone mounds, making for a surreal ride.*

▽ BELOW *The author looking extremely smug after surviving Slickrock.*

▽ OVERLEAF *Sandstone massifs, empty trails and clear skies – do not miss late winter in Utah.*

towards the La Sal ranges and over Amasa Back are surreal; enjoy them, as your eyes will be glued to the hairy singletrack once you hit the Portal downhill. Do not attempt this ride in winter, as ice and snow will make it an extremely dangerous mission.

Days three to seven take in the White Rim Canyon Trail. Canyonlands National Park, around 90 km (56 miles) from Moab, is home to this 160 km (100 miles) of unparalleled, multi-day mountain biking. Situated within the 'Islands in the Sky' section of what is Utah's largest national park, the trail generally takes three to four days to complete by bike. All your riding is along jeep tracks and gravel roads, traversing wild canyon country through areas such as Murphy's Hogback, Hardscrabble Hill and Mineral Bottom.

This is rated as a moderately challenging ride, but extreme caution is necessary, especially in mid-summer and during the freezing winter. Mountain bikers and other trail users have to make use of camp sites in ten designated areas along the route, and the number of trail users at any specific time is restricted.

DESCRIPTION: Three of the world's most famous trails, but dozens more await visitors to Moab.

ROUTE LENGTH AND DURATION: The featured rides vary from 16–160 km (10–100 miles), and may take anything from three hours to four days to complete.

WHEN TO GO: Summer is hot, while winter snow and ice will add to the level of danger, so autumn and spring are good. That said, February can have gorgeously clear days and means you will have nearly every trail to yourself.

SPECIAL CONSIDERATIONS: A full-suspension bike will improve handling in the gruelling terrain characterizing the Utah Desert. There are brilliant bike shops in Moab stocking quality hire bikes. Many of the trails require a high level of off-road skills, and there is a very real danger of injuring yourself if due care is not taken.

MAPS: Trail maps are freely available in Moab.

TOUR OPERATORS: Extensive operator/trail info is on hand at www.discovermoab.com.

PERMITS/RESTRICTIONS: These vary from trail to trail, and should be ascertained beforehand.

USA
San Francisco to Los Angeles

ALF ALDERSON

▽ *Big Sur – tough riding but worth the effort.*

The Pacific Coast Bicycle Route is a 2,956 km (1,836 mile) cycle trail that runs from Vancouver to the California/Mexico border. Is the San Francisco to Los Angeles section the icing on the cake? Well, that depends on what you like (wilderness lovers will probably prefer to be further north, for instance) but whatever the case this Adventure Cycling Association trail does give you the chance to see the essential California, from wild coastlines (Big Sur) to weird people (Venice Beach) and everything in between.

Where else to start but beneath the Golden Gate Bridge? Take your departure photos beneath this rust-red icon of west coast America, then turn your handlebars south and head for the sun – but not before exploring San Francisco first. This is one of the USA's most attractive and eclectic cities and reasonably bike-friendly; its famously steep hills will provide good preparation for the ups and down you'll encounter on your way south.

The route itself is both easy and hard; easy because the entire way is smoothly paved and well signposted – this is California, after all; hard because there's so much to stop off and gawk at *en route* that you can soon fall behind your schedule. And in purely practical terms you have to be aware that you'll be sharing the road with plenty of other users, most of them bigger than you. Although most major urban areas have good cycle paths, once out in open country you'll be on Highway 1, used by everything from logging trucks to RVs (recreational vehicles, or motorhomes), and whilst the road is wide enough and the drivers invariably civil enough to give you plenty of space, this won't appeal to everyone.

On the other hand, the highlights of the route will appeal to pretty much any cyclist. You're almost always within sight of the coast, so will be well aware if a big Pacific swell is rolling ashore – if so, take a short detour to Half Moon Bay on your first day's riding, since if the swell is big you might just see those few surfers who dare take on a 16 m (50 ft) wave known as 'Maverick' that breaks there.

△ *The Golden Gate Bridge, one of the most memorable starting points you'll ever find.*

△ ABOVE LEFT *Hippy culture is still alive and well in San Francisco.*

This proximity to the coast also allows you to cool down easily – there's no end of places along the way where you can jump off your bike and hop into the Pacific for a dip. And there's plenty of marine wildlife to observe, too, from the loud and smelly elephant seals at Año Nuevo State Park to sea otters and grey whales. Monterey is the easiest place to see wildlife, as boat trips will take you out to observe the whales, and the attractions here also include the world-famous Monterey Bay Aquarium on Cannery Row, although the rather twee tourist developments that dot the town are a long way removed from the gritty coastal settlement in which John Steinbeck lived and wrote of some 60 years ago.

Finding accommodation *en route* is rarely a problem (although it may be as well to book ahead in the busy summer season), with plenty of campgrounds, hostels and cheap motels, amongst which are some real one-offs, such as Pigeon Point Lighthouse, the second tallest light in the US, which is now a hostel.

facts and figures

DESCRIPTION: Quintessential California, from massive redwoods and steep hills to smooth, flat bike paths through eclectic towns and cities.

ROUTE LENGTH AND DURATION: 737 km (458 miles).

WHEN TO GO: Year-round, although mid-winter weather can be wet, especially in the north, and summer will be busy on roads and when looking for accommodation.

SPECIAL CONSIDERATIONS: Road bike/hybrid required. Tent and camping equipment optional. There is heavy traffic to deal with on many sections of the route.

MAPS: Available from the Adventure Cycling Association – email: tours@adventurecycling.org; web: www.adventure cycling.org

TOUR OPERATORS: Adventure Cycling Association (see above).

PERMITS/RESTRICTIONS: Waiver document must be signed to cycle through 17 Mile Drive in Carmel.

ACCOMMODATION: A wide range of campgrounds, hostels, motels and hotels are available along the entire route.

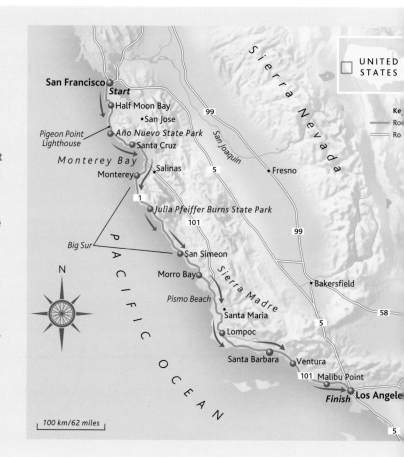

The undoubted highlight of the route is the very undulating section through Big Sur, where Pacific breakers crash against rugged cliffs, beyond which immense redwoods rise up from blue-green inland hills. It's well worth making a stopover here for a day to explore the coast at spots such as Julia Pfeiffer Burns State Park, or to hike up one of the inland trails to get a real feel for this magnificent landscape.

This is the hardest riding of the route – after Big Sur with one or two short exceptions, the terrain is easy, as is the living, for you're now entering the southern California of sand, surf and sun. Roll through Ventura County with warm sea breezes rustling the palms, cruise past Malibu Point and its designer homes, and maybe roll to a halt at weird and wonderful Venice Beach (not forgetting to lock your bike and remove your panniers!), which is about as 'LA' as you'll ever get, and in its own way just as memorable as the wild landscapes of Big Sur.

▽ BELOW LEFT *Bridging the gap through Big Sur.*

▽ BELOW *It's not all sunshine in California – heavy rain can create riding hazards.*

▽ OVERLEAF *The brilliant blue waters of the Pacific are an almost constant companion on this ride.*

CENTRAL & SOUTH AMERICA

"*Bright and fierce and fickle is the South.*"

Alfred, Lord Tennyson

△ *The grounds of Estancia Colomé in Salta, Argentina.*

From the Columbia–Panama border to Tierra del Fuego, South America is the fourth largest of the world's continents, covering an area of 17.8 million square kilometres (6.9 million square miles), and the fifth most populous, being home to some 380 million people in 12 countries. Here is the longest mountain range on earth, the Andes, stretching for a phenomenal 7,000 km (4,340 miles) from the Cordillera Oriental in Venezuela to Patagonia and Tierra del Fuego. The highest summit may be Aconcagua (6,962 m/22,835 ft) in Argentina, and the point on the earth's surface furthest from its centre may be Chimborazo (6,268 m/20,559 ft) in Ecuador, but there is so much more to the Andes. Many would argue that Alpamayo (5,947 m/19,506 ft) in Peru is the most beautiful mountain in the world, while others would point to the sensational rock sculptures of the Torres del Paine or Fitzroy in Patagonia. What is beyond dispute is the fact that the range is unsurpassed as a biodiversity hotspot, with over 3,000 species of plant, 1,000 species of amphibian, 600 species of mammal,

600 species of reptile and a staggering 1,700 species of bird. It is also accepted, in these days of global warming and climate change, that survival and protection of the tropical rainforests that used to encircle the entire northern Andes is crucial to the future of life on our planet.

Sadly, the experience of native South Americans with their Spanish and Portuguese colonizers in the 16th century was a good deal less than pleasant. The Conquistadores were merciless in their slaughter and relentless in their greed for the riches of the ancient civilizations they found. From their bases in Cuba, men like Hernán Cortés and Francisco Pizarro set out on orgies of pillage and looting that saw the Aztecs of Mexico and Incas of Peru liquidated in a matter of decades. Those who survived the onslaught of Spanish arms had then to contend with the smallpox and other diseases carried by their conquerors. Legends such as El Dorado spurred the Conquistadores on in their search for treasure, and the lure of such myths was powerful indeed. Sir Walter Raleigh took up the quest for Elizabeth I of England, and though his expedition up the Orinoco River in 1617 proved fruitless in terms of gold, he returned full of praise for what he had seen – "a country that hath still her maidenhood".

Such enthusiasm duly aroused the interests of more benign adventurers, and soon zoologists and botanists were thrashing their way into the rainforests of the South American interior. Baron von Humbolt spent a fruitful five years in the area from 1799, and his recognition of the link between cold water, warm air and the dryness of the Atacama Desert led to the ocean current flowing up the west coast being named after him. More famous still were the three voyages of the *Beagle*, the second of which, in 1831, had a passenger on board by the name of Charles Darwin. His book, *On The Origin of Species,* was published in 1859, and mankind's understanding of the natural world has never looked back since.

The sheer physical challenges involved in mounting expeditions to much of Central and South America would seem to preclude the humble bicycle as a means of transport, but in truth not all of this continent is mountain range and impenetrable rainforest. Much of Argentina and Chile and parts of Bolivia, Uraguay and Paraguay, for example, is pampas and steppes – home to that other icon of South America, the *gaucho*. The drinking of *yerba maté* is still as central to social ritual in these parts as drinking tea is to the English.

Cycling may not yet be central to the outdoor culture of South America, but this is rapidly changing – it is even Colombia's national sport. Perhaps inspired by the Bikecentennial in the US, two Dutchmen – Rob van der Geest and Wilbert Bonné – organized a similar ride in South America in 2008. Over a four month period riders completed an 11,000 km (6,820 mile) route between *Mitad del Mundo* ('Middle of the World') on the Equator in Ecuador, and *Fin del Mundo* ('End of the World') in Tierra del Fuego. If this seems ambitious, the rides that follow will certainly convince you of the potential for adventure biking in the land of the condor.

▽ *Cycling the Yungas Loop in Bolivia.*

MEXICO
The Yucatan Peninsula

IAN BENFORD

The Yucatan has much more going for it than its famous beaches and turquoise seas. Discover atmospheric colonial towns, striking Mayan pyramids and peaceful thatched hut villages. The land is dotted with underground lakes (*cenotes*) beneath the limestone plateau, the result of a massive meteor explosion said to have killed the dinosaurs. During March and April roads are often festooned with brightly coloured tree blossoms, making it a stunning place to cycle, while in the week before the Fiesta de Virgen de Guadaloupe (12 December) you can join long distance processions of cyclists. Carnivals in February and at Easter (*semana santa*) are also times of vibrant celebration.

▽ *The Ek Balam ruins north of Valladolid.*

Allow a week for this route, which offers undemanding cycling on paved roads. Starting in Merida, one of the oldest cities in Mexico, visitors can soak up the colonial culture, explore the markets and relax in the cafés around the tree-lined grand plaza. There is a wide choice of accommodation and restaurants. The first day's ride heads 110 km (68 miles) south toward the Puuc hills, passing picturesque old villages, *cenotes* and the Mayapan ruins. The journey to Tekit is on a new road, passing rustic settlements where children play and donkeys graze peacefully. The colonial town of Ticul offers a pleasant range of accommodation and restaurants where you can sample the local spicy cuisine. Or continue another 20 km (12 miles) into the hills to a lovely campsite just outside the peaceful village of Sta Elena.

On the 110 km (68 mile) circular route through the Puuc hills there are many incredible ruins to visit, including Uxmal (with its huge temple of the magicians), Kabah, Sayil and Labna (each with its unique architecture and hieroglyphs). Climbing into the hills offers splendid views over the plains below, and around the ruins the forest gives some welcome shade. The village of Sta Elena is worth a quick look if you haven't already been camping nearby, having a big church and a lot of character. To end the day, a tour through the fascinating caverns of Loltun is the perfect way to cool off and relax before the short ride downhill to Oxkutzcab. This pleasant town has a few hotels and a strong Mayan influence – many women wear the traditional *huipil* dress.

Next the journey heads northeast for 180 km (112 miles) to the colonial town of Tekax and on to Valladolid. This route is completely off most tourist itineraries, and for the next two days you get a chance to meet Latinos and Mayans in relaxed, natural settings. The journey can be broken in Peto, where there is basic accommodation. For more idyllic surroundings, ask locally to camp in Ichmul. This small village is stunning in its decayed grandeur, with two massive ruined churches and other colonial buildings surrounding a peaceful green area. On the first section the roads are busier, but after Peto, the number of cars per day can be counted on one hand. At the end of this route is the cool treat of a relaxing swim in the Dzitnap *cenote*. You can camp nearby with permission, or retire to Valladolid. This beautiful

△ *The inside of a ruined church at Ichmul.*

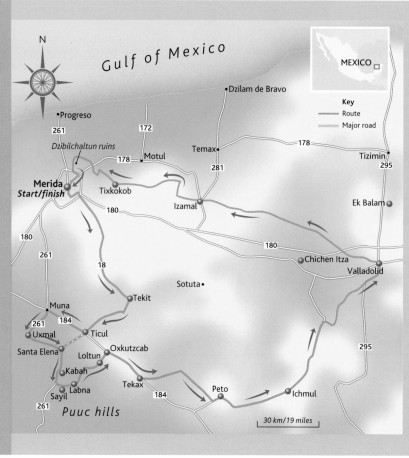

DESCRIPTION: Riding between charming colonial towns, majestic Mayan ruins and rustic villages, through the gently undulating low canopy forest where vultures soar above and butterflies flutter past on the midday thermals.

ROUTE LENGTH AND DURATION: Approx 560 km (347 miles), six days cycling.

WHEN TO GO: December–February. It becomes hotter toward April when the wet season begins.

SPECIAL CONSIDERATIONS: Any bicycle is fine – roads are all paved (with occasional potholes). Sunhat and sunblock are essential, and start early because of the heat. Carry at least 2 litres (half a gallon) of water, and carry some food because of the distances between shops.

MAPS: ITMB Yucatan Peninsular, 1:500,000 or Rough Guides Yucatan Peninsular, 1:500,000 (new roads are not included).

TOUR OPERATORS: None known, but check www.yucatantoday.com.

PERMITS/RESTRICTIONS: Entry fees for most Mayan ruin sites, and other attractions.

ACCOMMODATION: Hotels, hostels or camping.

colonial town has restaurants, hotels and the Zaci *cenote* within five minutes of the main square. There are excursions to the impressive Chichen Itza and Ek Balam ruins, if time allows.

The 80 km (50 mile) route to Izamal is very pleasant and peaceful, passing numerous Mayan villages and small colonial towns. The forest often laps the road edge, and later on the scenery opens out into grassland where white egrets mingle with the cattle.

Izamal is a delightful town, overflowing with a wealth of colonial architecture, painted in a warm yellow with Mayan ruins offering great views. There are several hotels and restaurants in the cobbled streets around the pristine squares. Returning to Merida, 80 km (50 miles) along the pretty side roads, the journey passes Tixkokob, the centre of Yucatan hammock production. Women can often be seen weaving in the villages on this route. The last leg heads to the north of the city to visit the Dzibilchaltun ruins and offers another opportunity to bathe in cool waters with a dramatic setting.

◁ FAR LEFT *Stone reliefs from the Labna ruins.*

◁ NEAR LEFT *Bici-taxis line up in Oxkutzcab.*

▽ *A shady road between Peto and Ichmul.*

COSTA RICA
La Ruta de los Conquistadores

PETER WALKER

Costa Rica is decidedly different from the rest of Central America, and proud of it too. While neighbouring nations have been mired in border wars and insurrection, the Costa Ricans formally abolished their military in 1949 and have happily made do without one ever since. The country is also blessed with an astonishing variety of natural beauty, all packed into an area only slightly bigger than Switzerland, about a quarter of which is national park. In fact, the great outdoors dominates life in Costa Rica to such an extent that much of its tourism – which employs around one in eight of the population – is based around adventure sports, whether trekking, white-water rafting or surfing.

▽ *Your reward: Costa Rica's laidback Caribbean coast awaits at the end of the ride.*

Plus, of course, cycling. There is no better way to experience everything the country has to offer than from the saddle of a mountain bike. There's also no better ride than a coast-to-coast epic, beginning on the rolling surf beaches of the Pacific edge and depositing you alongside the sultry mangroves of the Caribbean. It's ambitious; anything up to 350 km (217 miles) along tarmac roads, gravel paths and rutted mud tracks, not to mention a stretch of abandoned railway line complete with rickety wooden bridges across precipitous gorges. There's also the small matter of around 3,300 m (10,824 ft) of total climbing. But it's undoubtedly the most beautiful ride you will ever do, taking in tropical rainforest, coffee plantations, the rocky slopes of a (usually) dormant volcano and even a final stretch alongside a white sand beach.

Luckily, while the route is usually very quiet, it is also well established thanks to La Ruta de los Conquistadores, a famous annual mountain bike race set up 15 years ago by a group of local bike nuts. You can, of course, do the ride as part of La Ruta, held every November and open to enthusiasts as well as the whippet-lean pros. But rather than sprinting along in La Ruta's four breathless days, it's far more fun in, say, six or seven.

The trip starts in Jacó Beach, a bustling Pacific resort popular with surfers and holidaying families alike and a good base, with accommodation taking in everything from

△ *The Gandoca-Manzanillo nature reserve is only a short ride from the best post-trip rest stop, Puerto Viejo.*

DESCRIPTION: A four to seven day coast-to-coast tropical epic.

ROUTE LENGTH AND DURATION: The route is somewhat flexible, but reckon on more than 320 km (200 miles).

WHEN TO GO: The dry season runs from the middle to the end of November until April, when there will be less mud but prices are higher, especially around Christmas.

SPECIAL CONSIDERATIONS: A sturdy, well-maintained mountain bike with tyres ready for any condition should be used. No camping equipment is necessary as accommodation is plentiful. Pack a range of clothes – temperatures stay above 30°C (86°F) on the coast but it can get chilly in the mountains.

MAPS: There are many available, for example National Geographic's Costa Rica Adventure Map.

TOUR OPERATORS: There are many available – mountain biking is big business here.

PERMITS/RESTRICTIONS: None.

ACCOMMODATION: Numerous choices on either coast and plenty of hotels and smaller mountain lodges *en route*, for example in El Rodeo and Aquiares.

luxury resorts to backpacker fleapits. The first section of the ride is probably the toughest, as the climbing tarmac road disappears into red, gloopy mud. If it's raining, it's now you'll wish you'd gone in the dry season. Some pushing is inevitable, but enveloped in lush rainforest you really won't mind taking your time.

After skirting to the southeast of San José, Costa Rica's bustling capital (and the best mid-route detour for emergency bike parts), the path takes a decidedly uphill aspect – and keeps on going. The climbing eventually stops just below the peak of the Irazú volcano, taking you to just over 3,000 m (9,840 ft). Irazú isn't officially extinct, but it hasn't rumbled into action since the mid-1960s, so you should be fine.

Next comes the highlight of the ride for downhill speed junkies, as the bumpy, rock-strewn path from Irazú descends for mile after mile, the lush, green pastureland eventually replaced by acres of coffee plantations. The last stretch finally drops down from the central highlands, propelling you at top speed towards the Caribbean coast. Here, the heat gets steamier while

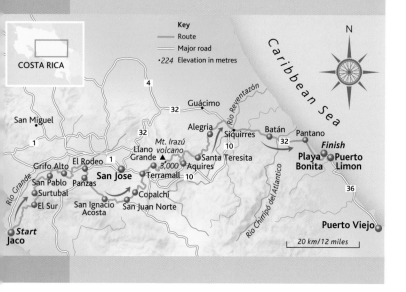

the surrounding culture shifts; a small but noticeable section of the population are of black Caribbean origin, the descendants of 19th century immigrant workers from Jamaica. You might even hear English spoken.

The next challenge is a section along a disused railway line between palm plantations, beautiful if slightly bumpy – the gaps between the sleepers have been filled in with rocks, but not very well. Then, just as you think you can hear the waves in the distance, the path turns sharply south, taking you along a sandy track for the last dozen or so miles, directly parallel to the beach.

The route officially ends in Puerto Limon, a bustling port town with plenty of hotels but little in the way of charm. You're much better off taking a bus – or riding, if you're not too stiff – another 60 km (37 miles) down the coast to Puerto Viejo, a laid-back strip of hotels, restaurants and ramshackle wooden beachside bars.

And once there? Well, just sit back with a cold beer and bask in the memories.

△ *Yes, it's a volcano. But don't worry, Irazú has been dormant for over 40 years.*

◁ *The Caribbean coast has everything you need for a relaxing holiday after your exertions.*

▽ OVERLEAF *Irazú's green crater lake. You can hike to near the very top of the volcano, assuming you have the energy.*

to complete it, and was the brainchild of the artist Leovigilda González who directed the artists from below with a megaphone. The mural symbolizes the theory of evolution. It's now been repainted in gaudy colours – a monumental piece of psychedelic art, or bad taste splotched on a rock face; it's a matter of personal taste. There's a restaurant at the base of the mural serving roast pork, rice, beans and virgin piña coladas – the perfect fuel to keep you cycling on into the afternoon.

The ride from Viñales heading roughly east towards the town of La Palma proves hard going compared to the gentle terrain of the Parque Naçional. There are lengthy stretches of isolated rural roads flanked by *mogotes* and palm trees. The potholes become more frequent and there are mammoth hill climbs in quick succession, but the reward is the white-knuckle ride down a 45 degree descent; what's known in these parts as *Loma del Americano* or 'American Hill'. This is exhilarating, if not terrifying, especially when approaching potholes at breakneck speed.

The journey ends at Cueva de los Portales, a dramatic hideaway that was Che Guevara's command post during the Bay of Pigs invasion and the Cuban missile crisis.

▷ FAR RIGHT *A tobacco shed just outside Viñales.*

▽ *Tobacco is grown in the rich red soil of the 'Garden of Cuba'.*

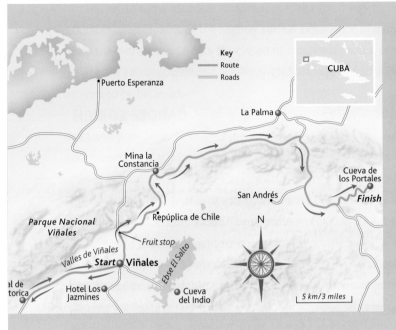

Key
— Route
— Roads

CUBA

Puerto Esperanza

La Palma

Mina la Constancia

Cueva de los Portales

San Andrés

Finish

Parque Nacional Viñales

Repúplica de Chile

N

Fruit stop

Valles de Viñales

Start Viñales

Ebse El Salto

Hotel Los Jazmines

Cueva del Indio

al de torica

5 km/3 miles

DESCRIPTION: Relatively easy road biking with the odd hill, but suitable for beginners.

ROUTE LENGTH AND DURATION: Approximately 80 km (50 miles), could be split between two days.

WHEN TO GO: Winter months are best (December–April). Avoid hot and humid summer months (June–August).

SPECIAL CONSIDERATIONS: Bike parts can be difficult to source if you aren't with a well-equipped tour operator. Be sure to bring snacks such as muesli bars, dried fruit and nuts – these are almost non-existent in Cuba.

TOUR OPERATORS: Cubania Travel (www.cubaniatravel.com) is the local tour operator, in conjunction with Exodus (www.exodus.co.uk) based in the UK.

PERMITS/RESTRICTIONS: There's a fee to visit the Mural de Prehistorica, but it's free if you have the pricey lunch at the nearby restaurant.

ACCOMMODATION: Hotel Los Jazmines is recommended.

facts and figures

Hidden deep in the Sierra del Rosario, this is no ordinary cave – a river flows right through the wall of mountains. Che's camp bed and desk remain untouched, and there was even once a telephone line.

There's an abundance of accommodation in or near the town. There are several good hotels and scores of *casas particulares*, which makes Viñales a great base for a cycling holiday. But arguably one of the best views of the valley can be seen from Hotel Los Jazmines, where you can recline in a rocking chair, rum cocktail in hand, and watch as the sun sets behind the magical karst peaks and the red soil fades into the evening. It's a well-earned reward after the steep hill climb to reach this magnificent view.

▷ *Taking a break near journey's end and looking back up towards El Rosal.*

▽ *Cycling through low cloud at El Rosal.*

▽ OVERLEAF *The road outside Subachoque.*

be predictable when giving you space. Many cyclists along the way will share a passion for riding – often overtaking you on a killing incline at speed without even appearing to sweat.

The route passes stunning forests and overlooks mountains hosting hundreds of small settlements, on a land that was an important sacred site for the wealthy Muisca Indians. Northeast of Sopo is Laguna Guatavita, the circular lake at the heart of this legend. 500 years ago Muisca King Zipa threw gold there as an offering to the gods. The probable cause of the Spanish myth of El Dorado, much of this has been recovered and is displayed at the Museo del Oro.

The road leads on to Zipaquirá, a town with some fine colonial architecture including an impressive salt cathedral and imposing green and white town hall. Its famous salt mines date back to the Muisca period and still contain vast reserves, despite intensive exploitation. This cathedral, which accommodates 8,400 people, has been a popular tourist attraction since 1954 although the town, which is named for the Chibcha word meaning the 'Land of Zipa', wasn't founded until 1606.

Those navigating the steep, challenging uphill climbs are rewarded by staggering views, such as that at Alta del Vino (2,715 m/8,905 ft) where stunning views of Bogotá spread through the distant valley like a child's miniature model. Further on are revealed vast panoramas of tiny wooden homesteads nestled in verdant plunging valleys, framed by the backdrop of velvety green-blue vegetation that crawls up the huge, craggy Andean mountains. The road passes through colonial-style villages; adobe-bricked settlements with heavy wooden shutters and doors, with tethered cockerels on the roadside. Much of Colombia's rich biodiversity is within easy sight, and as the route traverses mountain tops and valleys, the observant cyclist may spot eagles, woodpeckers and parrots as well as rare flowers such as orchids.

Although the gradients are formidable, the road surfaces are almost all paved. Even in the rain one can finish the route happily spattered and suffused with a sense of achievement and awe at the diverse beauty so close to this country's capital.

DESCRIPTION: A four day tour around northeast Bogotá including a number of very steep ascents.

ROUTE LENGTH AND DURATION: 230 km (143 miles).

WHEN TO GO: All year round.

SPECIAL CONSIDERATIONS: Road or touring bike required. Allow two days of acclimatization, stay alert for signs of altitude sickness, drink plenty of water and use sunblock. Wear clothing suitable for warm valleys and damp cold mountains, as you'll pass through both. While this route is perfectly safe it's inadvisable to wander alone in the dark or carry large amounts of money.

MAPS: www.colombiassh.org/site/IMG/png/Cundinamarca_A3.png has the best map.

PERMITS/RESTRICTIONS: None, although those not wanting to carry their luggage are advised to work around the availability of reputable support.

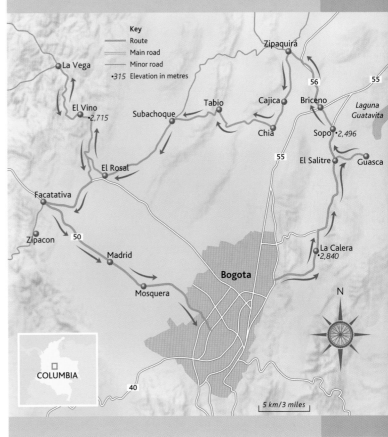

BOLIVIA
The Yungas Loop

LUKE WRIGHT

▽ *Take a couple of days to acclimatize before cycling at altitude.*

Looking at a map of South America, Bolivia is the little landlocked shape roughly in the centre – the heart of the continent. With the soaring wild peaks of the Andes quickly plummeting into the jungle's steamy insides, Bolivia is one of the most geographically and biologically diverse countries on the planet. Often only known for its connection to cocaine and as the resting place of Butch Cassidy and Che Guevara, Bolivia is, in fact, a traveller's hotspot. This country is at once an eye-opening, jaw-dropping, baffling and beautiful destination; an incredible place to explore and a highlight on the Latin-American Gringo Trail.

Bordering with Brazil, Paraguay, Argentina, Chile and Peru, this complex country, with a history of struggle and strife, is the poorest and most isolated in South America. The predominantly indigenous population is still closely tied to their ancient past: chewing the revered (and harmless) coca leaf, wearing colourful textiles and peculiar bowler hats, and worshipping the earth goddess, Pachamama. From the high, wintry altiplano down to the sweaty lowlands, Bolivia offers amazing and exciting experiences for serious adventurers and semi-soft travellers alike. It's cheap, mostly safe, and endlessly interesting. La Paz, Bolivia's cultural capital, is a sea of rooftops clutching to the sides of a vast valley plunging from the clouds. It's one of the highest cities in the world at approximately 3,650 m (11,972 ft) above sea level. The monstrous mountain, Illimani, watches from nearby, observing the city's unhurried and erratic pulse, as if standing guard while time unwinds for its residents. A dose of La Paz, its smells, sights, sounds and steep streets, is best taken with a good measure of time – to acclimatize to the altitude and to allow for the eccentricity of the city that touches the sky to take hold.

Bolivia, known as the Tibet of the Americas, is an incredible, world-class downhill biking destination, and this three day jaunt, starting from way up high just outside La Paz, takes in the best of the best. An epic cycle journey set in the magical mountains of South America, this route is not for those with a fear of heights. There aren't too many places on the

planet where cyclists can climb into the saddle at a literally breathtaking (and freezing!) 4,750 m (15,580 ft) mountain pass and rarely need to touch the pedals until hours later at a balmy 1,100 m (3,608 ft) on the edges of the Amazonian basin. But it's all possible on the Yungas Loop.

△ *A head for heights is a* *necessity on this route.*

DESCRIPTION: From the clouds to the lowlands, a three day journey with lots of downhill action.

ROUTE LENGTH AND DURATION: Approximately 209 km (130 miles), three to four days.

WHEN TO GO: May–September – avoid December–March due to rain.

SPECIAL CONSIDERATIONS: Take a reliable, sturdy mountain bike and clothing for snow and sun. Be aware that altitude sickness is a serious concern and that this ride can go from snow to sunshine very quickly.

TOUR OPERATORS: This ride is best taken with a tour group and support vehicle. www.gravitybolivia.com is by the far the best, most experienced and most reputable operator.

PERMITS/RESTRICTIONS: Entrance fee.

ACCOMMODATION: There is guesthouse accommodation in each town: Adventure Brew Hostel in La Paz, Sol y Luna in Coroico and El Castillo in Chulumani.

Day one begins from the eye-watering, hand-freezing heights of La Cumbre (4,750 m/15,580 ft) to Chuspipata (2,100 m/6,888 ft). The first section is 22 km (14 miles) of downhill delights on a sealed and wonderfully winding road amid a dramatic backdrop of massive mountains. From here this back-to-basics expedition plummets down, down, down, in the shadow of the giant Andean peaks, into what the Inter-American Bank once dubbed the world's most dangerous road – a rather grim title for what is an incredible, fun-filled ride. This section finishes up in Yolosa (1,100 m/3,608 ft), where it's best to take a taxi or bus up the hill to the sunny town of Coroico (1,700 m/5,576 ft) – a good place to stay for the night.

Day two is a tough cross-country excursion through the coffee, coca and banana growing region of Bolivia, traversing rarely used roads and encountering life in Bolivia as it has passed for many hundreds of years. It's hard not to smile riding in these parts, passing through what feels like an authentic slice of Bolivian life. The day ends with a very challenging ascent to Chulumani (1,580 m/5,182 ft) where a bed and a hot meal awaits – a welcome respite for sore legs and hungry stomachs.

After a well-earned rest in Chulumani, day three is an up and down affair that makes its winding way next to a spectacular raging river gushing with icy Andean water. After a day by the roaring river, the ride culminates at the oddly out-of-place El Castillo ('The Castle'), a surreal and apparently haunted castle situated at 1,952 m (6,403 ft). El Castillo offers food and accommodation and it's worth spending the night here in this strange location. From El Castillo, buses regularly make the journey back up into the clouds of La Paz.

△ *El Castillo is an atmospheric and slightly spooky place to stay.*

◁ ABOVE LEFT *The Yungas Loop provides world-class downhill cycling.*

ARGENTINA
Salta

CAROLE EDRICH

▽ *The border between the Cactus Park and Estancia Colomé.*

This land of *gauchos* and tradition has it all: gorgeous green villages, winding silver rivers, deep red canyons, vertiginous vermillion *arroyos* and some of the most desolately beautiful land in the world. Named *Salta La Linda* ('Salta the Beautiful') by the Argentines, the impressive Andes form a constant backdrop, and the combination of altitude, switchbacks, *ripio* (loose sharp gravel), sand and all-pervasive dust makes a challenging but rewarding ride. Much of this route follows the partially paved Ruta 40, traversing the verdant Valles Calchaquíes and the desolate Puna Salteña salt flats and high passes before slowly descending to Cafayate.

One of the wildest and least travelled roads on the planet, Ruta 40 runs parallel to Argentina's Andean spine. Regarded by locals with affection and awe, it was travelled by Che Guevara and featured in the film *The Motorcycle Diaries*. It runs from the border with Bolivia in the north, through Salta, down to the southern land of glaciers. From Salta (1,190 m/3,903 ft) the first turn of Ruta 33 ends as a long straight run through Parque Naçional Los Cardones. This 65,000 ha (160,550 acre) expanse of dry uplands rising from 2,700 m (8,856 ft) to 5,000 m (16,400 ft), with a distant backdrop of stratified candy-pink rock, is home to the candelabra cactus, or *cardon*, some of which can live for 300 years. Riding amongst these legendary giant sentinels with arms thrust up to the vast cloudless sky is an extraordinary but challenging experience, as this desert reserve has no stops for supplies.

The alternative route via San Antonio de los Cobres is arguably the highest in Latin America. Steep inclines at altitude lead to switchbacks through the stunning Quebrada del Toro gorge and San Antonio de los Cobres (4,180 m/13,710 ft) and the route descends along less steep but equally challenging declines and a fantastic panorama at Abra de Acay (4,900 m/6,072 ft) before joining Ruta 40. The rewards are tremendous, as the route reveals expanses of dirty yellow scrub and the brilliant white salt flats of the Puna. The horizons are edged by pastel-coloured mountains and profusely dense forests, before you descend through tiny hamlets of neat adobe houses shrouded in low cloud, which clears to give dramatic views of breathtaking valleys and velvety bronze-green mountains.

Ruta 40 crosses Cachi (2,280 m/7,478 ft) at the foot of the nine-peaked Nevado de Cachi, in a wonderfully verdant valley irrigated by channels built by Diaguita Indians long before the Incas arrived. Before Molinos (2,000 m/6,560 ft) it passes close to Quilmes; here you will find important archaeological ruins of a pre-Inca town, through villages of handsome colonial architecture and churches with roof beams and confessionals of *cardon*.

▽ *Vineyards at Casa de la Bodega, located at the start of the valley of Quebrada de Las Conchas.*

South of Molinos is the extraordinary Estancia Colomé. One of the most exclusive luxury boutique hotels in Argentina, this oasis of cultivation is a fully biodynamic farm and excellent winery boasting hectares of pre-phylloxera vines. The route's southward stretch passes more vineyards, becoming easier on the pass through Quebrada de las Flechas ('Gorge of Arrows'), comprised of high, dark cliffs eroded into toweringly sharp peaks jutting aggressively into the bright blue sky. It descends through areas of exquisite natural beauty; tiny villages with whitewashed churches, green fields and orchards where tenacious inhabitants have for centuries scratched a living from the dry desert soil.

This voyage of discovery ends close to Cafayate on Ruta 68, in a 60 km (37 mile) round-trip investigation of Quebrada de las Conchas ('Gorge of Shells') and its valley. Dawn is the best time for both wildlife and photography. Ñandúes (ostrich-like rheas), caranchos

facts and figures

DESCRIPTION: A 12 day arduous but non-technical trip in northwest Argentina, with the option of a number of incredibly rewarding diversions.

ROUTE LENGTH AND DURATION: 670 km (415 miles) and 11 days (via Ruta 33 and Ruta 40). Extension via Ruta 78 and Ruta 48 adds eight additional days.

WHEN TO GO: All year round, but wash-outs can occur between February and April.

SPECIAL CONSIDERATIONS: Thornproof tyres, mountain bike or hybrid. In general, ascents are slow enough that you'll acclimatize as you go, but be alert for signs of altitude sickness. Carry water everywhere and use strong sun protection. Food and water stops are scarce, the wind can be fierce, there is often no shade and mobile phone reception is rare. The alternative route via Punta del Obispo should be undertaken with a guide. Take warm clothes, emergency drinks and a blanket in case you become stranded at night. Confirm any planned rail travel with the railway provider itself, as the trains run to a particularly Latin schedule!

MAPS: Argentina YPF Guide, A4 magazine: Tourismo Salta.

TOUR OPERATORS: Acampar, Turismo Cordilerano, Salta and Cafayate Tourist Offices.

ACCOMMODATION: Casa de la Bodega, Patios de Cafayate, La Casa de Los Vientos, Hosteria de Angastaco, Cardones de Molinos, Colomé, Hotel Solar de la Plaza.

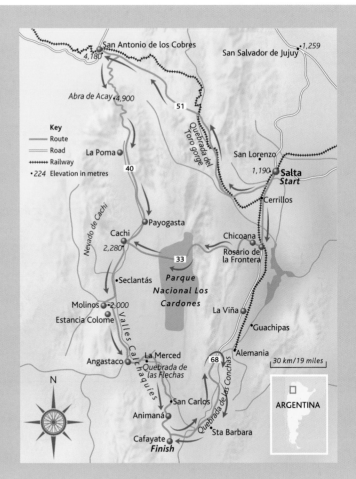

and condor are amongst the birds to be found. Exposed formations beautifully eroded by heat, wind and rain, the rich greens of the valley, a silvery river and ochre, pink, burgundy and terracotta canyon walls form idyllic scenes revealed anew with each twist of the road. El Anfiteatro is a natural amphitheatre with acoustics good enough for regular outdoor concerts, and Los Castillos ('The Castles') and El Sapo ('The Toad') are formations particularly worth seeing.

350 days of sunshine, a high thermal amplitude and fantastic *terroir* have produced some excellent, intensely red wines and the white Torrontes for which the region is famed. Those in the know relax in the shade at San Pedro de Yacochuya overlooking sun-drenched, lavender-laden gardens and vineyards, discovering in their fruity, dry Torrontes a delicious combination of strength and excitingly light floral aromas, and the sense of a hard ride well done.

▽ *Las Ventanas ('The Windows') at Quebrada de Las Conchas.*

▽ OVERLEAF *Moonrise over the Salteño Desert.*

ARGENTINA
Welsh Patagonia

CAROLE EDRICH

△ *The verdant Trevelin Valley.*

In 1865, invited by the government of Argentina, around 160 Welsh people set sail for a new life in South America. After a voyage of considerable hardship in the harsh Patagonian winter they landed at Punta Cuevas, which today lies on the outskirts of Puerto Madryn. The colony slowly grew until increasing competition for land and difficult seasons forced a group of horsemen (*Los Rifleros*) to explore inland. This route follows their journey up the River Chubut to Esquel and Trevelin, a fertile land quite similar to Wales where they settled and prospered.

On the first day, most riders choose to follow Ruta 2, the coastal route to Peninsula Valdes which passes El Doradillo Beach. This ride provides the opportunity to watch southern right whales who gather here to mate. It then traverses the isthmus separating the San José and Nuevo Gulfs and ends at the Interpretation Centre at the entrance to the nature reserve of Peninsula Valdes, where elephant seals, hairy sea lions and Magellan penguins may be found.

The route proper, which follows Ruta 25 almost exclusively, starts back at Puerto Madryn, passing Trelew, Gaiman and Dolavon before crossing a section of the endlessly horizoned rolling Patagonian plains and gradually ascending from Las Plumas to Paso de Indios. It then takes a slow descent past Teka where it joins the legendary Ruta 40 for the trip through Esquel to Trevelin. Although the majority of the route is well surfaced with paving or concrete, caltrap-shaped thorns will cause three or four punctures each day unless proper precautions are taken.

Welsh Patagonia is not a myth or an invented tourist attraction. Hundreds of its inhabitants speak Welsh, and far fewer speak English. Welsh language and history is taught in schools and annual Eisteddfodau and other music, song and dance festivals have been held since the first settlers landed in 1865. Once through Puerto Madryn and Trelew, many take advantage of the wonderful Welsh teas to stoke up their energy for the coming days'

△ *The outskirts of Esquel as seen from the ascent from its valley.*

DESCRIPTION: Exploring Argentina's central Patagonia, from the coast through the interior to the Andes foothills.

ROUTE LENGTH AND DURATION: 850 km (527 miles), 15 days.

WHEN TO GO: Avoid April and May as winds in these months can gust at up to 193 kph (119 mph). Whale season at Puerto Madryn is June–December.

SPECIAL CONSIDERATIONS: Hybrid or touring bikes and thornproof tyres. Carry full camp kit, food and water. While the roads are often paved, winds can be strong and there are very few places to stay.

MAPS: Argentina YPF Guide, Footprint Argentina.

TOUR OPERATORS: Ski Patagonia or contact LATA.

PERMITS/RESTRICTIONS: Fee of around $5 for entrance to national parks in Puerto Madryn and Los Alerces.

ACCOMMODATION: Santa Rita, Libertador, Unelem, Casa de Piedra Chacra Labrador, Tehuelche and Casa Verde Hostal, and camp sites at Las Chapas, the Florentino Ameghino dam, Las Plumas, Los Altares and Paso de Indios.

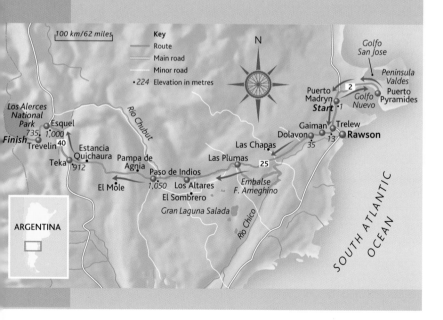

rides. Such teas are probably an innovation of recent generations, as their abstemious ancestors were unlikely to sit down for a snack of several different scrumptious cakes, bread and scones at one sitting!

Dovalon's water wheels were used to raise water for irrigation for decades and have been left in their old positions for aesthetic and historical value. Founded in 1915, and meaning 'river pasture' in Welsh, this town grew from hitching post to important hub for coast-to-Cordillera trips, thanks to the arrival of the railway. For several kilometres from here the route passes through rocky headlands, forming an orange-red canyon around the Chubut river bed. Those who choose can climb the steps up to landscape observation posts to view the sandy river banks, deep vegetal greens and sparkling water that contrast with the walls of the canyon itself. Tehuelche cave drawings and petroglyphs can still be seen at Las Plumas, which was mined by the tribe who inhabited this land for thousands of years for its aragonite, red jasper and coffee-coloured chalcedony (a type of quartz).

The long and arduous journey of *Los Rifleros* ended just south of Esquel, where Butch Cassidy and the Sundance Kid lived in a hideaway home until allegedly robbing the local bank and moving on. *Los Rifleros* crested a high ridge obscured by fog which eventually cleared to reveal a huge fertile valley. Cwm Hyfryd ('Beautiful Valley') is set before the majestic snow-clad Andes and is where Trevelin ('Mill Town') is now located. An old mill-turned-museum illustrates the town's settlement and history, and it's clear that the Welsh and Tehuelche mixed together with a measure of success. Their trade in rhea feathers (a bird rather like an ostrich) was at one time more profitable than gold, and they subsequently became a major supplier of wheat to Argentina. They now export cherries to Marks and Spencer in the UK and bulbs to Holland.

Fog, rain and mist are inevitable in this area, and together with the language create a sense of central Wales. Despite this no trip would be complete without a final, quintessentially South American, leg to Los Alerces National Park to see the mountains bordering Chile and the Alerces trees that have grown there for 2,500 years.

◁ *A local cyclist on a ripio surface near Trevelin.*

▽ *Puerto Madryn at dusk.*

▽ OVERLEAF *The route into Esquel, the town made famous by Butch Cassidy.*

EUROPE

*"The bicycle is the most civilized conveyance known to man.
Other forms of transport grow daily more nightmarish.
Only the bicycle remains pure in heart."*

IRIS MURDOCH

△ *Stunning views of Sussex from Blackcap on the South Downs Way in England.*

From the Arctic Ocean to the Mediterranean Sea and from the Atlantic Ocean to the Bosphorous, Europe is not so much a continental landmass in itself as a huge peninsula of Eurasia. It is the second smallest of the continents, after Australia, with an area of just under 10.4 million square kilometres (4 million square miles) and a population of approximately 731 million people living in 47 countries.

In many ways Europe leads the world with its enlightened attitudes to cycling, and the incorporation of dedicated facilities for cyclists in town and transport planning in both rural and urban contexts. The governments of Holland, Denmark and Germany in particular have long realized the benefits of cycling both for the health of their people and the development of urban centres as pleasant places to live and work. Integrated cycle paths and lanes, the modification of road intersections, traffic calming measures, the provision of bike parking and its co-ordination with public transport, the education and training of both car drivers and cyclists and the implementation of traffic laws enforcing cyclists' rights have all combined to make European cities the most bike-friendly on the planet.

These measures, implemented over the last three decades, have given Europe the right to boast both the highest levels of bike use and the lowest levels of accidents involving cars and bikes in the world. In Holland today there are two bikes for every member of the population and cycling accounts for 27 per cent of all journeys, whilst in the USA the figure is just one per cent and the fatality rate per mile ridden is over five times higher.

Sport cycling has similarly long held a central place in the European consciousness. The first organized bike race, in 1892, was the Liége–Bastogne–Liége, over a gruelling 260 km (161 mile) return route in the Belgian Ardennes. This event – also known as *la doyenne* ('the oldest') is still held annually today. And it is, of course, the Tour de France – or simply le Tour – that is the most famous cycling race in the world. First conceived by journalist Géo Lefévre as a publicity stunt to boost the flagging sales of the newspaper for which he wrote – *L'Auto* – it has been held, with the interruption of two world wars, every year since 1903. In that first event, 60 riders set off from Montgeron for the 19 day, six stage, 2,500 km (1,550 mile) ordeal. Le Tour has never been for the faint-hearted. The longest stage in the first race was a herculean 471 km (292 miles) from Nantes to Paris, and it is perhaps unsurprising that Maurice Garin crossed the finishing line to win the tour ahead of only 21 others.

The total distance covered by le Tour varies every year (the longest was 5,700 km/ 3,534 miles in 1929), but the average is 3,500 km (2,170 miles). Many of the participants over the years have become household names the world over – men like Eddie Merckx, Miguel Indurain and Lance Armstrong. The race leader's yellow jersey and the King of the Mountains' red polka-dot jersey are as renowned as the names of some of the more famous stages and landmarks passed in the mountains.

The routes described in this chapter include several of these – the Col du Tourmalet on the traverse of the Pyrenees, for example. Whether you wish to test your fitness and time yourself over these formidable passes or simply enjoy the magnificent mountain scenery on the way, these are classic rides in every sense. Elsewhere you may sample the technical challenges of the West Highland Way in Scotland, explore Bohemia in the Czech Republic or marvel at the astonishing Amalfi Coast in Italy. No section of this book offers a wider variety of terrain, climate or cultural diversity. You may think you know Europe, but these rides will surprise even the most seasoned traveller. What are you waiting for?

▽ *Nearing the summit of Col de Peyresourde in the Pyrenees.*

ENGLAND
The Yorkshire Dales

SALLY HOWARD (WITH THANKS TO MARK ALLUM)

From the dramatic limestone outcrops of Malham Cove and Gordale Scar to the flower-carpeted meadows of Swaledale and Dentdale; from the shadowy peaks of Whernside and Ingleborough to the deep valleys carved by river flow that give the region its name, the Yorkshire Dales make for some of the most spectacular mountain biking in Britain.

▽ *High above Dentdale.*

△ *Descending into Crummackdale.*

And now's the time to go. Cycling is blossoming across the Dales, thanks in part to forward-thinking pub owners who – inspired by the old English tradition of horse liveries – have instituted a number of pit-stops attached to pubs, where cyclists can wash, repair and house their cycles undercover during an overnight stay (a feature unique to the area). The Dales' drowsing villages and bustling ancient market towns also offer a profusion of cyclist-friendly cafés and pubs, as well as world famous ale breweries for those confident of their poise on bike-back.

The region's chief draw, however, is its shifting terrain: high, open moorland and grassland with long climbs and descents and bike trails that traverse, contour and fall away into frequent valleys – offering all the theatre of a mountain riding experience without the physical demands of more remote peaks. And, with over 800 km (496 miles) of bridleways, byways and green lanes, there's a bounty of possible routes. The following five-day tour takes in the region's highlights.

Day one takes you from Reeth to Hawes. Start at Reeth town, the meeting point of two of the Dales (Swaledale and Arkengarthdale). Head into Arkengarthdale and take the bridleway over Reeth Low Moor to Fore Gill Gate. Continue past the remnants of Old Gang smelting mills and mines to the sweeping descent from Gunnerside Gill, which segues into an effortless trail to Gunnerside town. Cross from Swaledale to Wensleydale past Crackpot and Summer Lodge, and enjoy a bridleway descent to Woodhall. Scythe through lush Wensleydale to conclude your day in at the White Hart Inn, Hawes (which offers a cycle livery).

▷ *Coming down the Craven Way to Ribblehead.*

On day two you'll cycle from Hawes to Austwick. Climb out of Hawes on the West Cam road track, drinking in the wraparound views. Then either cycle straight down the Cam High Road to Ribblehead or – for a longer day – take the Pennine Bridleway down to Newby Head to descend Arten Gill (a new section of the bridleway opened in spring 2009). Continue down Dentdale, joining the Craven Way – a superb old packhorse route with a stunning descent to Ribblehead. Pick up a short section of tarmac down to Selside and continue along Long Lane for limestone scenery at its best: the flat limestone carpet of Runscar scar, striated with deep clefts by centuries of running water. Take in the muscular arches of Ribblehead viaduct in the distance before dropping down into the village of Austwick, and a warm welcome at the Wood View bed and breakfast.

Day three, and it's Austwick to Grassington. Leave Austwick via the ancient stone clapper bridge and follow the Pennine Bridleway through to Settle and beyond. An inching

facts and figures

DESCRIPTION: A circular route taking in the highlights and contrasting topography of the Yorkshire Dales.

ROUTE LENGTH AND DURATION: Around 180 km (112 miles), depending on route choice, five days.

WHEN TO GO: Accommodation for one night could be difficult to find in the middle of summer, so spring and autumn are advisable.

SPECIAL CONSIDERATIONS: Take a mountain bike, 20–30 litre rucksack and the usual spares.

MAPS: OS Explorer OL2 and 30, or Harvey Maps series of the Dales.

TOUR OPERATORS: Dales Mountain Biking organize two trips a year, see www.dalesmountainbiking.co.uk for details of this and their new self-catering accommodation.

PERMITS/RESTRICTIONS: None.

ACCOMMODATION: Hawes, The White Hart Inn (www.whiteharthawes.co.uk); Austwick, Wood View B&B (www.woodviewbandb.com); Settle, The Royal Oak, site of the first bike livery (www.royaloaksettle.co.uk); Skipton, The Tennant Arms, Kilnsey, with cycle livery (www.tennantarms.co.uk).

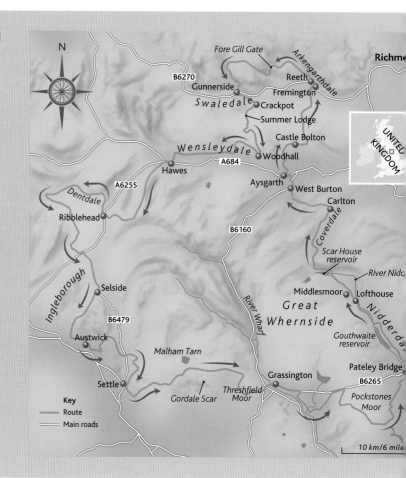

climb up Stockdale Lane (steel your nerves with a good breakfast) approaches an easy descent towards Malham Tarn. Then it's along the old Roman and monastic route of Mastiles Lane, branching off for an exhilarating run down Threshfield Moor to Grassington and the Yew Tree House bed and breakfast.

Grassington to Lofthouse or Middlesmoor is the plan for day four, involving a languid start to the day on back roads before a breathtaking route over Pockstones Moor and a long, fast descent into Nidderdale to Pateley Bridge – an old lead mining region where you can still spy the grassed-over depressions of old mining shaft heads. Work your way up the valley following its series of cycle tracks, past the glittering shard of Gouthwaite reservoir to the head of the valley, breaking at Lofthouse or Middlesmoor.

On day five, return to Reeth. The riding is more technical for this epic concluding day, which loops you back to your starting point. From Middlesmoor a track with fabulous views leads over the moor to a snaking descent down to Scar House reservoir. Cross the dam and mount Deadman's Hill to reach Coverdale. Then from Carlton a slow climb up leads to a swooping, breath-defying descent alongside Thupton Gill. As you pass through West Burton and Aysgarth, stock up on supplies for your final climb back into Swaledale, its foot at the glowering, medieval Castle Bolton. The newly opened Dales Mountain Biking Centre's accommodation in Fremington, just outside Reeth, will piece together weary bikes and limbs.

ENGLAND
The South Downs Way

ADAM MONAGHAN

Starting in Winchester and running over 160 km (99 miles) of bridleways through Hampshire and Sussex to the finish in Eastbourne, the South Downs Way is a classic English mountain bike ride. With the route skirting past some significant natural landmarks and picture-perfect villages, this really is as English as England gets.

Whilst the ride can be completed in a day (think about averaging 11–16 kph/ 7–10 mph), such an endeavour will require some serious preparation. One website lists this route as only for 'very experienced off-road riders', and with a significant proportion of the 3,100 m (10,000 ft) of climbing appearing towards the end of the ride leading in to

▽ *The green, green grass of England, and the view that greeted the 1994 Tour de France peleton as they crossed Ditchling Beacon.*

Eastbourne, you really must have your climbing legs on. Of course, all this ascending means an equal amount of descending, and the South Downs Way features plenty of fast downhills; you can expect to see the clock hit 64 kph (40 mph) on a number of occasions.

Of course, being England, the biggest challenge is the weather – and up on the Downs there is simply no hiding from it. If you are very fortunate, a gracious tailwind will blow you to Eastbourne – the angle of the trees is a good example of the prevailing wind tendencies. Although there are odd patches of woodland, most notably nearer Winchester, the majority of the riding is very exposed, so set out well prepared for all conditions – that means sunblock *and* waterproofs! Inevitably, rain changes the entire feel and pace of the ride. Being so overtly made of chalk, the descents and climbs quickly become rutted by running water in wet weather. And even on flat, rolling sections, the wet chalk can become a challenge in itself. Wet chalk is like ice. No, really. Let me say that again: wet chalk is like ice. You have been warned!

With the bridleway doing its best to cling to the top of the Downs, there are not a huge number of amenities available along the path itself. However, there are a few water taps to refill bottles and with each drop down and the inevitable encounter with civilization, there is usually a pub or a village shop to replenish supplies.

△ *Pick the right time of year and you'll be treated to glorious yellow fields of rape around Kingston Ridge.*

▷ *An uncommon piece of shade on one of the numerous climbs between Alfriston and Eastbourne.*

▽ *On clear days, Firle Beacon offers stunning views across Sussex to the north and out to sea to the south.*

▽ OVERLEAF *The dividing line between agriculture and nature and an extremely rare strip of concrete along the top of the Downs.*

By hitting the tarmac at Ditchling Beacon and heading south along Ditchling Road, the relative metropolis of Brighton can be reached within minutes. Indeed, with its numerous hotels, bars and seafront cafés it may be the ideal place to stop if you are planning the journey over two days. Since the South Downs Way also crosses the main A27 road a little further along, it is also a very easy place from which to pick up the trail again the following day. Other bed and breakfasts and campsites can be found by ducking off the trail at any number of places, but be sure to make advance bookings. And note that, as the land is designated National Park land, camping on the Downs is not permitted.

The final signposted descent into Eastbourne sadly means you actually miss Beachy Head, and after 160 km (99 miles), you may not be too inclined to ride back up to see it (although at 162 m/531 ft it is the highest chalk sea cliff in Britain, so it's worth a look). However, by veering to the right and heading south after crossing East Dean Road and then hopping onto the road for a couple of kilometres, you can very easily get to the top. If you need more motivation, there is a pub and an ever-present ice cream van! From the top you can take any number of paths or either of the two fast road descents to get back onto the seafront.

There are numerous organized events that involve the South Downs Way, if that appeals – the British Heart Foundation Randonnée is probably the most popular and will require early applications (December/January applications for May/June events). Trailbreak also run a through-the-night event, starting in Eastbourne at sunset and racing the sun to Winchester. There is even a South Downs Way 24 Hour Double (Eastbourne–Winchester–Eastbourne) for those feeling truly masochistic!

DESCRIPTION: 160 km (99 miles) of bridleways through woodland, rolling hills and chalk cliffs in classic English countryside.

ROUTE LENGTH AND DURATION: 160 km (99 miles) including 4,150 m (13,612 ft) of climbing and descending. It can be completed in one day (8–14 hours) or spread over two to three days.

WHEN TO GO: In winter the chalk becomes treacherous and many parts are so slippery or churned up as to be unrideable. Daylight is also a serious consideration for one-day attempts. Aim for May to September and cross your fingers for good weather!

SPECIAL CONSIDERATIONS: It is not a technically demanding route but a mountain bike is the essential tool. You'll need to take enough food and water to get you to the next road crossing or village and enough tools to keep your bike going. Take clothes for all conditions and be prepared for close encounters with livestock! The bridleway is widely used by walkers and horses so do be courteous.

MAPS: The route is mostly very well signposted, so keep an eye out for the blue arrows and acorns on gate posts. Or take Harvey Maps – South Downs Way XT40 edition.

TOUR OPERATORS: British Heart Foundation (www.bhf.org.uk) or Trailbreak (www.trailbreak.co.uk).

PERMITS/RESTRICTIONS: None.

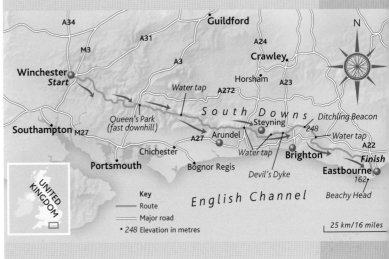

SCOTLAND
The West Highland Way

JON SPARKS

A bell? On a mountain bike? No, honestly. On a route like the West Highland Way, popular with walkers, it's the friendliest way of announcing your approach.

The bell's no joke, and neither is the Way. Rolling out from Milngavie at the edge of Glasgow's sprawl, all seems tame enough, but within an hour or two the route begins to show its teeth. At Balmaha you cross the Highland Line, a major geographical and cultural boundary. Ben Lomond, the southernmost of the Munros (defined as peaks over 3,000 ft/ 915 m), looms above and the broad lower reaches of Loch Lomond are squeezed into a tapering ribbon.

▽ *Two views of the trail beside Loch Lomond.*

△ A descent before
Inversnaid, looking north
over Loch Lomond.

Ross Wood offers a taste of things to come: bikes on shoulders up rocky steps, then a descent spiced with hefty drop-offs and sneaky drainage gaps. Some you can roll over, some need a smart bunny-hop, and one or two demand trials skills. It's all avoidable, but soon there will be no soft option.

Rowardennan has a hotel, a youth hostel and a feeling that it's the point of no return. An easy forest track suckers you in and then it gets rough: Ross Wood to the power of ten. The strong and technically adept may be able to ride most of it; some trials gods might ride it all – but I'll believe it when I see it. For mere mortals it's a mix of riding, pushing, carrying and moments when it feels awfully like rock climbing, packed into 2 km (1 mile) that can take an hour or more.

The sudden appearance of the hotel at Inversnaid feels like an alien craft has just landed. It's a good spot to regroup, but there's more rough stuff to come – at least as much again, and probably more. Opposite Rubha Ban, the Way becomes mostly rideable again. Civilization beckons, first with the ferry (summer only) to Ardlui, then Beinglas campsite. It's not even halfway, but the toughest part is over. And let's just observe, at risk of heresy, that if the hike-a-bike really puts you off, you could catch the train to Ardlui, catch the ferry and still do the most inspiring stretches of the Way.

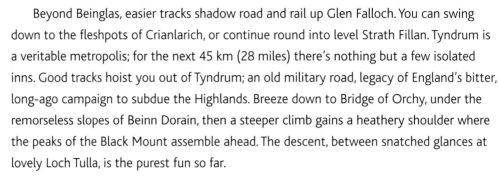

▷ *Singletrack near Lochan Lùnn-Dà Bhrà, on the final stage.*

▽ *A stile interupts the flow on the final stage.*

▽ OVERLEAF *An old drovers' road near Kingshouse, with Buachaille Etive Mor behind.*

Beyond Beinglas, easier tracks shadow road and rail up Glen Falloch. You can swing down to the fleshpots of Crianlarich, or continue round into level Strath Fillan. Tyndrum is a veritable metropolis; for the next 45 km (28 miles) there's nothing but a few isolated inns. Good tracks hoist you out of Tyndrum; an old military road, legacy of England's bitter, long-ago campaign to subdue the Highlands. Breeze down to Bridge of Orchy, under the remorseless slopes of Beinn Dorain, then a steeper climb gains a heathery shoulder where the peaks of the Black Mount assemble ahead. The descent, between snatched glances at lovely Loch Tulla, is the purest fun so far.

An old drovers' road climbs gradually to 445 m (1,460 ft) on the skirts of the Black Mount. To the north stretches the vast, sodden chaos of Rannoch Moor. Hitting the descent, a minor detour takes in the White Corries ski centre, which stages downhill mountain biking in summer, and serves monster bowls of fries. Or rattle on by, gazing at the climber's dream peak, Buachaille Etive Mor. The Kingshouse Hotel is the last refuelling stop before the crunch climb of the Devil's Staircase. It's all rideable, but you'll need to be good. Topping out at 548 m (1,797 ft), it's virtually all downhill to Kinlochleven at sea level, and most of it is an absolute feast. Rarely can you lift your eyes to the hunched ridges of the Mamores, the Aoanachs and the Grey Corries. Finally, easy tracks skim into Kinlochleven, the last rest stop before the Way's end.

Climbing away from the loch is tough, especially straight after breakfast. Then a wider track, another old military road, rises more amenably to 335 m (1,099 ft) at Lairigmor – the big pass. Framed by regular slopes, the track sweeps away fast and inviting. Climb over grassy knolls above Lochan Lùnn-Dà Bhrà, and Ben Nevis shoulders massively into view before singletrack twists down into forest. Just as it starts to feel trail-centre cosy, a steep wooden staircase reminds you this is primarily a walkers' route. Little swoops and stubborn rises reach a crest near Dún Deardail hill fort. Now it's all downhill; a final flourish of snaky singletrack, then a fast forest road and tarmac for the last gasp, or grin, into Fort William.

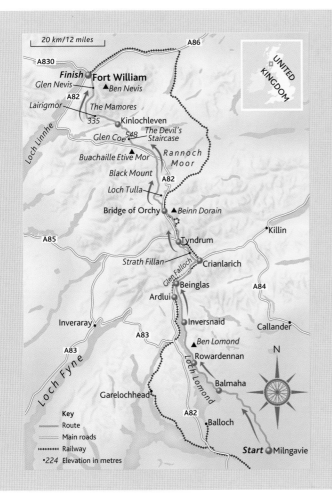

DESCRIPTION: A tougher-than-expected route taking in rocky woodland and exposed hill slopes amid magnificent mountain scenery.

ROUTE LENGTH AND DURATION: 153 km (95 miles). Has been done in a day, but best over three. Highest point: 548 m (1,797 ft).

WHEN TO GO: Spring–autumn. The northern part of the route is used for motorcycle trials in early May (see www.ssdt.org).

SPECIAL CONSIDERATIONS: Start at Milngavie (Virgin Trains to Glasgow then Scotrail local service); finish at Fort William (Scotrail back to Glasgow). Mountain bike (and skills) essential; a good hardtail is easier to carry on day one than a full-susser! No bike shops between end points. Busy with walkers in July and August. Midge repellent essential June–September.

MAPS: Harvey Maps XT40 West Highland Way is excellent and well worth taking with you.

TOUR OPERATORS: No specialist bike tour operators, but walkers' services will carry baggage – just do an internet search for 'west highland way baggage'.

PERMITS/RESTRICTIONS: None.

ACCOMMODATION: A wide range, from campsites and wilderness shelters to hotels.

145

SWEDEN
Hoga Kusten

JACQUES MARAIS

▽ *Rough riding is on the cards if you take on the trails in the Skuleskogen National Park.*

If deep forest cranking is your thing, programme Sweden's Hoga Kusten ('High Coast') region into your travel planner right away. Here, along the northeastern shoreline of this striking Scandinavian country, a riot of multi-day mountain biking routes and quick-fix trails await the many members of the fat-track tribe.

A major land uplift (up to 285 m/935 ft in places) has shaped this hilly region along the shores of the Baltic Sea, thus creating a World Heritage Site featuring remarkable geological and botanical variety due to its comparatively recent emergence from below the oceans. Ecosystems vary from northern Boreal and western Oceanic to Alpine relic forests, with woodlands clinging to windswept uplift headlands, or proliferating on marine detritus deposits. All of which will be largely irrelevant to you as you blast downhill through the emerald haze on a singletrack trail more suited to a cliff-dwelling tahr than mountain bikers. Hardcore cranking is certainly not your only option along Sweden's High Coast, though, as numerous villages dot the coast between the towns of Harnosand, Kramfors and Ornskoldsvik.

A first-world network of tarmac roads, dirt tracks and cycling trails join these scenic villages, offering the perfect environment in which to explore the Hoga Kusten, either on your own or as part of an organized bike tour. The High Coast Trail, renowned as one of Scandinavia's premium hiking routes, offers an excellent route for mountain bikers as well. The northern gateway to the High Coast Trail is Ornskoldsvik ('vik' translates to 'bay', and is how the Vikings of yore got their name). From O-vik, as the town is known to locals, cyclists can roughly follow the trail southwards, all the while planning daily stopovers and route terrain to suit their personal level of fitness and skill.

On day one, a 36 km (22 mile) crank takes you via Svedje and Sandlagen to Kopmanholmen. If off-road riding blows your hair back, days two and three should be planned so as to allow at least two nights in the Skuleskogen National Park. To fully explore the dramatic topography of the park, some of the trails must be tackled on foot, especially if you want to explore Slattdalsskrevan and the high viewpoints overlooking the Gulf of Bothnia.

The forest trails here are luminescent with light, with wraparound rays colouring shimmering leaves and textured bark in a dappled glow. In the distance, the staggered trunks of birch shine like pale pickets against a veil of chartreuse, jade and olive green. Pine needles and leaf matter blanket the trail, cushioning the sound of your advance amidst a riotous profusion of undergrowth all round. Hundreds of metres above the current sea level, you emerge from the trees onto *klatterstenn-feldts*, or heaped fields of rounded boulders also known as 'The Devil's Pasture' because very little life can be coaxed from them. These shingle or moraine fields demarcate the earlier edge of the ocean, which recedes by approximately 1 cm (0.4 in) each year due to ice melt and the corresponding isostatic land lift.

▽ *Scenic villages line the route as you traverse the High Coast Trail.*

Near the summit of Skuleberget, sparse Alpine vegetation and stunted pines eke out a tenuous existence. Here you'll find Slattdalsskrevan, a gargantuan gash ripping across the summit as if some powerful Viking god smote the mountain in two with his mighty broadsword. More than 200 m (656 ft) long, 40 m (131 ft) deep and in places only 6 m (20 ft) across, this mythical cleft leads onto red cliffs plummeting hundreds of metres to a verdant tableau of sparkling lakes and islands. This rates as one of Sweden's blue chip views, all the more so if you can enjoy it at dawn or dusk.

Continue onwards from Skuleskogen on your journey southwards, aiming to reach Ullanger by the end of day four (a ride of approximately 30 km/19 miles). Finally, day five leaves you with a leisurely 16 km (10 mile) crank to Hjornoberget and the end of a glorious ride along the Hoga Kusten's shoreline. It is important to note that the 127 km (79 mile) trail can be completed over any number of days, and that daily distances will depend upon your route choice and the terrain you are cycling across.

◁ *Relishing the ride along the High Coast.*

facts and figures

DESCRIPTION: A coastal cycle, following roads and trails traversing the rugged Bothnian Gulf.

ROUTE LENGTH AND DURATION: 127 km (79 miles), with daily legs varying from 15–36 km (9–22 miles).

WHEN TO GO: Early summer through to mid-autumn (May–September) mean extended daylight hours and perfect cycling weather.

SPECIAL CONSIDERATIONS: If you plan to follow the actual High Coast Trail for most of the way, a dual suspension bike will add to the overall comfort of the ride. If you stick to the tarmac, the route will constitute a markedly shorter road ride. Sweden subscribes to the concept of *Allemansrat*, or freedom to the great outdoors for all. You can therefore take your tent and set up camp just about anywhere you want along the trail.

MAPS: Quality maps are available from sport shops in Ornskoldsvik.

TOUR OPERATORS: Active travel, such as hiking and biking, is a speciality of www.hikebike.se. Also check out the bike hire and accommodation deals from www.reklasa.se.

PERMITS/RESTRICTIONS: None – Sweden is forward-thinking when it comes to ecotourism, and allows recreational adventurers maximum freedom.

ACCOMMODATION: Camp wild along the trail, or stop at any of 12 designated stop-over points.

CZECH REPUBLIC
Bohemia

JACQUES MARAIS

▽ BELOW RIGHT *Trailing through the forests above Marianske Lazne.*

▽ *Historic architecture, great beer and a blend of culture and leisure options make Prague one of the world's most gorgeous cities.*

Bachelor parties and statuesque blondes are big on the menu for many tourists visiting the Czech Republic, but if this is what spikes your heart rate, you're reading the wrong book. Be that as it may, it's a good bet that you'll enjoy riding your bike more than trawling clubs anyway. Bombing the trails in this ex-Communist country is as about as good a ride as you'll get, and options cover all the bases from tarmac cruising to cranking the sweetest of singletrack. Most of my riding in the Czech Republic has been up in the Cesky Les Forests around Marianske Lazne (also known as Marienbad), with dozens of day rides from the pretty village of Lazne Kynzvart keeping us in the saddle for more than a week.

Towering pines and a mix of evergreen giants loom skywards along the steep ridges shucking up towards Lesny Peak (983 m/3,224 ft), and there are endless trails traversing the surrounding slopes here. Best of all, the trails are tamped, perfectly bermed and super-smooth, guaranteeing you a trail-riding blast along a truly unforgettable network of swooping singletrack.

Marianske Lazne and the fantasy forests of Cesky Les offered so much to explore that we did not get around to any of the Czech Republic's glorious multi-day rides. I did, however, research the options while in the country, and the trail described here, from Cesky Krumlov to Prague following the Vltava River, is the one I plan to return for.

Set off on this week-long trip from the village of Cesky Krumlov, a UNESCO Heritage Site right on the edge of the sumptuous Sumava National Park. Guided groups will be met at either their hotel or the airport for the transfer from Prague, allowing enough time to explore the medieval town on the first day. The ride kicks off on day two, meandering along off-road biking trails and country roads through the scenic valley of the Vltava River.

△ *The Bohemia region rates as one of the true off-road riding paradises in Europe.*

The degree of difficulty is moderate, and the 42 km (26 mile) first stage allows enough time to explore Ceske Budejovice and have a beer or two here, in the home town of Budweiser. On day three, an early start from Hluboka nad Vlatou sees you taking on a 55 km (34 mile) stretch via Tyn and on to Pisek. Tranquil lakes line the route, and an ancient stone bridge in Pisek, dating back to the 13th century, makes for a fitting end to the day's riding.

Day four (45 km/28 miles to Zvikovske Podhradi) and day five (50 km/31 miles onwards to Pribram) will take you past romantic castles and many a picturesque village. Pribram itself has been a mining centre since the Middle Ages, but has a dark side to its history – during the Communist era, political prisoners were forced to work on the uranium mines here.

Saddle up on day six, continuing towards Karlstein, a ride of 46 km (29 miles) along the Sierra Trail through the Brdy Forests. This may prove to be either the most challenging or

▷ *Evergreen giants dwarf mountain bikers along one of the scenic Cesky Les trails.*

most exciting day of your trip. Off-road trail options abound, with calf-crunching climbs and white-knuckle downhills for those keen on testing their bike skills. The bravest of the brave will take on the hard slog to the top of Stozec (600 m/1,968 ft), but this is not compulsory.

From Karlstein, it is an easy 32 km (20 mile) cruise to Prague, the breathtaking capital of the Czech Republic. The route along the Vltava and Berounka riverbanks takes you right to your hotel, and you should plan to spend at least three nights in what surely rates as one of Europe's most dreamy cities. The people are friendly and easy on the eye, while the Budvar (or Budweiser) beer is surprisingly affordable. Walk on the historic Karlovy Bridge, visit Prague Castle, lunch in the Old Town Square, and revel in the exquisite mix of ancient Europe, Communist chic and breathtaking architecture.

DESCRIPTION: Perfectly tamped forest singletrack and cycle trails along winding forest roads make for sublime biking.

ROUTE LENGTH AND DURATION: 270 km (167 miles), or around 32–55 km (20–34 miles) per day.

WHEN TO GO: Glorious weather during spring, summer and autumn means you should aim to do this trail any time from April through to October.

SPECIAL CONSIDERATIONS: Even though some of the riding will be off-road, the terrain is suitable for bikes *sans* suspension. Except, of course, if you plan to take on the singletrack. If you cannot bring your own bike, expect to pay 200–500 CZK per day when hiring a bike on a daily basis. Operators generally supply bikes on multi-day tours.

TOUR OPERATORS: Contact local experts Ave Bike Tours at www.bicycle-tours.cz.

PERMITS/RESTRICTIONS: Cycle routes are well signposted; look out for yellow signboards.

ACCOMMODATION: Self-catering accommodation is extremely affordable, especially in the smaller towns and villages. Enquire at the local tourism offices for a list.

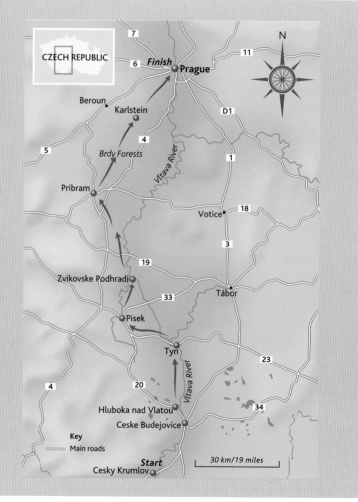

SLOVENIA
The Julian Alps and the Soca Valley

ROBIN MCKELVIE

When Austrians and Italians flock across the border to savour your mountain scenery, you know you have something special – and Slovenia certainly does boast something special. This tiny republic is home to some of the most dramatic mountain landscape in Europe, awash with skyscraping peaks, tumbling rivers and gleaming Alpine lakes, making it perfect adventure sports and cycling territory. Long distance cycling in Slovenia is still in its infancy, as most locals prefer a quick half or full day jaunt. The country, though, is ideal for longer adventures, with a stunning panorama waiting around every corner, plenty to see and do *en route* and characterful places to stay.

▽ *A cyclist in Voje Dolina, a side-trip from Bohinj.*

Kranjska Gora, the country's premier ski resort, offers easy access to the legendary Vrsic Pass and is an ideal starting point. The pass is a rewarding challenge for cyclists. Built by Russian prisoners in World War I, it spirals deep into Slovenia's protected Julian Alps with no fewer than 50 hairpin bends to negotiate. Happily, 26 of them are downhill.

The effort of pedalling up is well worth it, as craggy peaks rear up on all sides. *En route* to the top, sights to look out for include the poignant Russian Chapel, dedicated to the prisoners of war who lost their lives here, and sparkling Lake Jasna. Keen walkers won't want to miss the chance to sneak off at the top of the pass on one of the hiking trails. Easing down the other side of the Vrsic, the road becomes smoother and the gradients flow in cyclists' favour on the sweeping descent down Route 206 into the verdant Soca Valley, in Slovenia's Primorska region. The eponymous River Soca is a milky blue rush of adrenaline that provides grade five thrills for white-water rafters and kayakers alike. The small town of Bovec makes for an ideal first night stop, with adventure sports on hand or just cosy inns and restaurants geared to the needs of those who have been out braving the elements on a bike all day.

Breaking south from Bovec, the road winds its way along the Soca, with some opportunities to take to quieter riverside tracks. Cyclists today ease down the valley glad

△ *Stunning mountain scenery is a highlight of this trip.*

that, unlike their ancestors, they don't have to engage in the bitter mountain warfare that claimed the lives of a million souls here in World War I. Between Bovec and Kobarid a number of stretches of the old front line trenches remain as a moving testimony to their suffering. The award-winning Kobarid War Museum is unmissable, offering a real insight into those dark days. Kobarid these days has a lighter side, too, with a sprinkling of top-notch restaurants that attract Italian gastronomes from just across the border. The highlight is Topli Val, where you can enjoy fresh trout simply grilled or in a variety of inventive permutations.

Pushing on south down Route 102, the next overnight stop is in the small village of Tolmin. The great attraction here is outdoor sports, so if you didn't get out on the waters in Bovec you can kayak, raft or even hydrospeed here, the latter a river version of bodyboarding. The country's best bungee jump is also nearby for real adrenaline junkies.

The next day the cycle back north looks a daunting one, with a hulk of mountains to tackle. Help is at hand, though, as a 'car train' runs through the mountains from Primorska into the Gorenjska region and the lakeside resort of Bohinj, the base for the third night. Bohinj is home to a picture-perfect glacial lake fringed by trees, ideal for lazing around and easing tired muscles.

▽ Lake Bled, with the castle on the right.

DESCRIPTION: A great route around the Julian Alps and the Soca Valley.

ROUTE LENGTH AND DURATION: 168 km (104 miles), four days.

WHEN TO GO: Avoid November–May as the Vrsic Pass is often badly affected by snow and closed completely. June and September are usually the best months weather-wise, with relatively dry and mild weather.

SPECIAL CONSIDERATIONS: A mountain bike or a good hybrid is required. Heavy rain and cold temperatures can be problems at any time of year, so the correct gear should always be carried.

MAPS: Freytag Berndt – Slovenia.

TOUR OPERATORS: Helia Travel Agency can organize a trip on this route as well as shorter and longer itineraries. It is also possible to arrange transfers through them to avoid steeper climbing sections. See www.cycling slovenia.com for more information.

PERMITS/RESTRICTIONS: None, though a nominal fee is sometimes charged to enter the Triglav National Park.

ACCOMMODATION: Hotel Kanin in Tolmin, Pension Rutar in Bohinj and Hotel Bohinj in Bohinj.

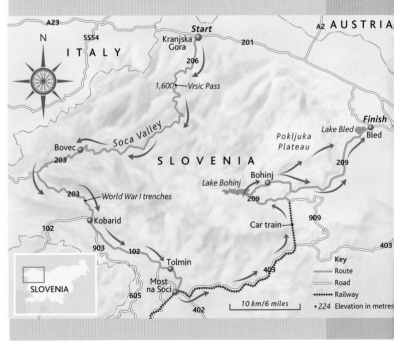

For the last day there is a much more interesting ride from Bohinj to Bled than on the main road – instead, take the route up onto the Pokljuka plateau that revels in all sorts of Alpine flora and fauna as you cycle in a scene framed by vaulting Julian Alps peaks.

Journey's end comes when you descend into Bled, a resort home to not only the prettiest lake in Slovenia, but perhaps in Europe. Cycling by the lake as the bells of the island church chime across the still waters is a sublime way to finish your adventure. After four days cycling around the Julian Alps and the Soca Valley, you will now appreciate just why Austrians and Italians flock to enjoy one of Europe's least heralded but most enthralling cycling destinations.

▷ *The view from Mont Aigoual.*

▽ BELOW RIGHT *Cyclists on the Canal du Midi.*

▽ *Saint Guilhem le Desert.*

was carved 6,000 years ago by the River Vis. The long descent and subsequent climb from the Cirque can be avoided by returning to the road to Madières. The route becomes easier along the cool woodland valleys of the Herault, as you cycle towards the unrivalled magnificence of Saint Guilhem le Desert and the evening's lodgings at Saint Jean de Fos.

Life starts to get more gentle as you bowl along surrounded by the world's largest wine producing area. Amble through the village of Arboras, climb towards the Col du Vent and turn off the route towards La Roquette and Saint Martin. You'll pass by Octon and Lac du Salagou, where you can take a detour into the curious Cirque de Mourèze. Descending the Orb Valley, with its vines on one side and craggy Espinouse mountain range on the other, is a real cycling pleasure. If you have time, explore the narrow hillside routes; there is plenty of scope for adventurous detours. Crossing the river bridge south leads to a lush, vine-rich valley and Roquebrun, an exquisite town in which to pass the night.

The final day forges onward through the vines and St Chinian – one of region's most renowned wine producing areas. The countryside undulates as you pedal across the patchwork landscape of vines, olive trees and cyprus trees. Ahead are hills and plains stretching to the Pyrenees and the impressive village of Minerve, perched on its rocky outcrop. The journey ends by joining the world-famous Canal du Midi at Trebes and making a triumphant entrance to Carcassonne – the proud gatekeeper to Cathar country.

DESCRIPTION: A traverse of Languedoc Roussillon, from the medieval town of Uzès through the vines, high Cevennes, deep gorges and Canal du Midi towards the majestic splendour of Carcassonne.

ROUTE LENGTH AND DURATION: 510 km (316 miles) over five days (but could be lengthened depending upon your appetite to explore).

WHEN TO GO: Spring or autumn – avoid the heat of summer or the snow-topped hills in winter, and watch out for the strong winds and rains of autumn.

SPECIAL CONSIDERATIONS: A road bike with good climbing gears is needed. Uzès can be reached by bus from Nimes, and Carcassonne and Nimes are linked by train.

MAPS: Michelin Maps' regional map of Languedoc Roussillon for overall view, Michelin local maps or IGN maps for fine detail.

PERMITS/RESTRICTIONS: If you plan to cycle further on the Canal du Midi, written permission is required from Canal authorities in Toulouse.

ACCOMMODATION: Each day is planned to end in towns with lodgings.

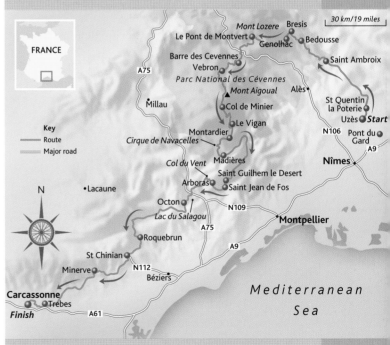

FRANCE

30 km/19 miles

Key
— Route
— Major road

Mont Lozere · Bresis
Le Pont de Montvert · Bedousse
Genolhac
Barre des Cevennes · Saint Ambroix
Vebron
A75
Parc National des Cévennes · Alès
▲ Mont Aigoual
St Quentin la Poterie
Millau · Col de Minier
Uzès **Start**
Le Vigan
Montardier · N106 Pont du Gard
Cirque de Navacelles · A9
Madières · Nîmes
Col du Vent
Saint Guilhem le Desert
Arboras · Saint Jean de Fos
Octon · N109
Lac du Salagou · Montpellier
·Lacaune · A75
N Roquebrun · A9
St Chinian
Minerve · N112
Béziers
Mediterranean Sea
Carcassonne · Trebes
Finish · A61

FRANCE
The Pyrenees

MAX WOOLDRIDGE

Running with the bulls in Pamplona, flying a fighter aircraft in Arizona – both adrenaline-rich, high-octane experiences that this author has relished – but neither are as exhilarating as hurtling down a Pyrenean mountain road at 97 kph (60 mph) on a racing bike. With sheer drops on one side, only bike-handling skills and brake pads stand between you and certain death.

Starting at Foix, near Toulouse, set off along quiet valley roads following the Areige River gorge before hitting the Pyrenean foothills and a gentle ascent of the second-category Col de Port, down to Seix. You won't be far from the town of Lourdes, the popular tourist town in the Pyrenees, but on this trip you will be a pilgrim come to worship a more tangible god. Your sacred domain is the famous cols – or mountain passes – of the Tour de France, culminating in the Col de Tourmalet, at 2,115 m (6,937 ft), the highest road pass in the Pyrenees.

▽ BELOW RIGHT *A cyclist in the village of St Lary heads towards the Col du Portet d'Aspet.*

▽ *Views of the Ariege countryside near Seix.*

Out of Seix, hit the Pyrenees proper with the Col de la Core. This first category climb will bludgeon you in the face like a sledgehammer, and no amount of soaking your bandanna in cool mountain streams will help lessen the savage gradients. But once you reach the high meadows near the top, a huge sense of achievement will outweigh any pain. A delightful descent takes you past sleepy towns and the clinking sound of old men playing boules. Drink a refreshing Orangina at a local café, where you may well notice your arms are mottled with dead flies, drowned in suntan lotion and sweat.

The next morning will provide a sobering reminder that even professionals get it wrong sometimes. Halfway down the impossibly steep Col du Portet d'Aspet, a memorial salutes the Italian former Olympic champion Fabio Casartelli, who died here after a gruesome downhill crash in the 1995 Tour. From the Col de Mente, ascend the Col du Portillon, a mountain pass that straddles the French and Spanish borders, towards the lively spa town of Luchon. Unwittingly, this is one of the funniest towns in France, thanks to its mix of health and hypochondria. While Luchon is a magnet for the active, elderly French ladies straight out of Beryl Cook cartoons also gather here for the thermal baths you can smell miles away.

Luchon is the ideal place for a rest day, but Superbagneres – a ski station at 1,800 m (5,904 ft) sometimes used as a Tour stage finish – may prove too tempting. Set off in the early morning before the sun gets too fierce. As you pedal up the long and steady climb through the picturesque Valley de Lys, you will soon become locked in your own private torment. When the air becomes noticeably cooler and you hear the clanking cowbells of

▽ *Sunshine and clouds at the summit of the Col de la Core.*

DESCRIPTION: An unforgettable cycle trip in the Pyrenees over the some of the most famous mountain passes of the Tour de France.

ROUTE LENGTH AND DURATION: Approximately 403 km (250 miles), six days.

WHEN TO GO: May–September. Avoid winter as the cols will be closed.

SPECIAL CONSIDERATIONS: Bring camping gear if you don't plan to stay in hotels, plus spare inner tubes for your bike. Use a road or mountain bike with plenty of gears. Take a supply of snacks for when shops are shut and sunblock.

MAPS: Michelin maps number 235 (Midi-Pyrenees) and 234 (Aquitaine).

TOUR OPERATORS: Exodus run a Classic Cols of the Tour de France cycling holiday that follows a similar route, starting in Tarascon, based in St Girons (www.exodus.co.uk).

PERMITS/RESTRICTIONS: None.

ACCOMMODATION: There are lots of campsites, hotels and guesthouses *en route*.

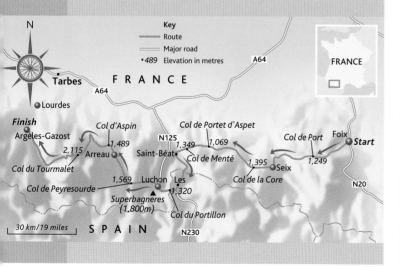

cattle, you will know that you are near your goal. Once again, any agony will be forgotten at the top.

Each day on this route follows a wonderful routine. Wake to the gentle sound of birdsong and the peeling of village church bells, sleeping at night on U-shaped mattresses in small hotels, eating hearty meals of pasta, *confit de canard* and *foie gras*. Every morning will throw up another challenge, usually visible from your hotel window.

Out of Luchon the following day, a glorious descent of the Col de Peyresourde takes you to Arreau, where grey slate roofs contrast with bright lycra. You will soon be back in your lowest gear, grovelling up the winding roads and hairpin bends of the first category Col d'Aspin. The names of Tour riders are painted on the road and special signs reveal the gradient and distance left to the summit. These mountain passes are little short of paradise. Cars wait until there is a straight stretch of road in which to overtake – unthinkable behaviour in the UK, where cyclists are public enemy number one. Overnight in St Marie de Campan, a sleepy village nestling in the shadow of the Tourmalet.

This giant of the Pyrenees is certainly tough – and unmercifully steep in places – but you will find it strangely easier than expected, conditioned by your previous efforts. The summit heralds superb views; bright blue skies surrounded by soaring Pyrenean peaks like broken teeth. You will want to stop and celebrate your achievement, but may well find it too chilly to hang around for long. The 32 km (20 mile) descent to Argeles-Gazost is an intensely memorable downhill. As you enter the warm valleys below there will be no finish flag or *maillot jaune,* just an immense sense of euphoria. But also a sense of dread – what experience on a bike could ever top this?

◁ *The author reaches the top of the Col d'Aspin.*

▽ *A sign near the top of the Col du Tourmalet shows its severe gradient.*

▽ OVERLEAF *Three cyclists approach the summit of the Col du Tourmalet.*

FRANCE
Burgundy

SALLY HOWARD

▽ *Cycling with a backdrop of Château de La Rochepot.*

Burgundy is a timeless area of France. In the region's fiercely proud villages, old men idle over boules or a piquant local *epoisse*, and the passage of seasons is measured by the ripening of the grapes of the world's most famous vintners that blanket the panorama as far as the eye can see.

Largely uninterrupted by traffic, you'll cycle along snaking vineyard tracks, through fragrant woods and cobbled medieval towns and past magnificent palaces and centuries-old châteaux. The best time to visit is *vendange*, or harvest time, when butterscotch sunshine slants down on the locals at their quick-fingered work and all hands and toes are stained a vivid purple. This four day ride begins gently, the terrain becoming hilly on day four, but there's the perfect antidote to pedal-weary legs in a glass of chocolatey local red. Raise your glasses to *un séjour agréable*!

Begin in Dijon, at the Château de Saulon-la-Rue, a sprawling 17th century vineyard estate crouching in winebottle-green forest. The going's easy. Scythe along the broad Saône River plain through fluttering wheat fields and rustic farms to the village of Vougeot and continue on to the famous Burgundy *grand cru* estate of Clos de Vougeot – where monks first planted vines in the 12th century – drinking in the view as you lunch beside the glittering River Vouge.

You'll need to refuel for the afternoon ahead: an inching uphill progress to the Hautes-Côte de Nuits, part of the Côte d'Or limestone ridge (and the feature that gives the Burgundies their distinctive characteristics). The legwork will be worth it for the view, and the exhilarating downhill to Gevrey-Chambertin, a sleepy village whose environs are home to eight *grand cru* vineyards. Meet the gently undulating, vineyard-flanked route to the village of Chambolle Musigny and the luxurious 18th century Château André Ziltener, where tasting professionals are on hand to take you through the hotel's fabulous cellar.

Shake off your *grand cru* fog on day two and pedal south, following the Côte d'Or through vineyards and the town of Nuits St-Georges to the walled medieval Beaune, a city with the atmosphere and good looks of a village. Bounce through the city's cobbled streets and pick up a crisp local take on the classic French *croque-monsieur* (or the meaty local *escargot* if you've worked up an appetite for the exotic) before continuing on through the vineyards, or exploring the network of caves cut out of the rocks beneath Beaune. Spend the night in the city, perhaps dining in one of Beaune's candlelit cave restaurants.

Breakfast heartily on day three, then continue into the Côte de Beaune (the southern sweep of the Côte d'Or). Follow vineyard and forest trails, gliding toward the chocolate box village of La Rochepot and down into the heart of another jewel in Burgundy's crown: the Montrachet, the *grand cru* vineyard that's said to produce the best white wine in the world. Explore the famous wine villages of Puligny, Chassagne and Meursault and continue through Volnay and Pommard before looping into Beaune to spend the night at the Hôtel Le Cep, housed in a collection of townhouses around a courtyard that date back to the middle ages.

▽ *The third day's riding takes you through the beautiful village of Volnay.*

△ *The lush and hilly Valley de l'Ouche.*

▷ *Cycling past a vineyard in the Côte de Beaune.*

Start day four by riding from the Côte de Beaune northwest into the Ouche Valley. The landscape is immediately spectacular – rolling hills, quiet country roads and the sleepy villages of Nantoux and Mandelot. The rugged riding segues into the flat Vallée de l'Oche, where the going is easy and you can contemplate dining at your hotel for the night, the Michelin-starred Abbaye de la Bussière in La Bussière sur Ouche, a chateau set in a 7 hectare (18 acre) park.

On day five, wind through the valleys and farms surrounding the Abbaye to the top of the village and famous castle of Châteauneuf. This impeccably preserved medieval site dates back to the 12th century and is regularly voted the prettiest village in France. Bounce along the cobbles, stopping for lunch at a café, before continuing through the village to the trip's dramatic conclusion – the downhill run to Les Jardins de Barbirey, a fabulous 19th-century garden.

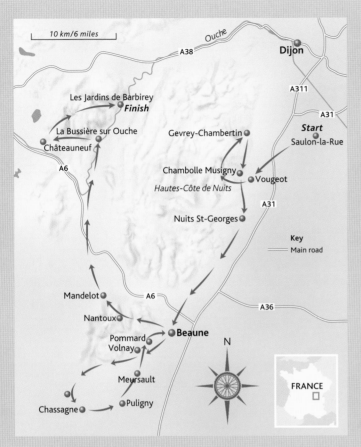

10 km/6 miles

Ouche

A38

Dijon

A311

A31

Les Jardins de Barbirey
Finish

Start
Saulon-la-Rue

La Bussière sur Ouche

Gevrey-Chambertin

Châteauneuf

A6

Chambolle Musigny

Vougeot

Hautes-Côte de Nuits

A31

Nuits St-Georges

Key
—— Main road

Mandelot

A6

Nantoux

A36

Pommard
Volnay

Beaune

N

Meursault

FRANCE

Chassagne

Puligny

DESCRIPTION: A route through some of the best-known vineyards in the world: Charmes-Chambertin, Morey Saint-Denis, Musigny and Romanée-Conti.

ROUTE LENGTH AND DURATION: Five days. The biking is easygoing to moderate. Average daily biking distance is 40 km (25 miles).

WHEN TO GO: September to catch the harvest, but this route is pleasant in spring, summer and autumn.

SPECIAL CONSIDERATIONS: Take a hybrid or road bike, plus a helmet.

MAPS: The Michelin map of Burgundy.

TOUR OPERATORS: Butterfield & Robinson (www.butterfield.com).

PERMITS/RESTRICTIONS: None.

ACCOMMODATION: Château André Ziltener in Chambolle-Musigny, Hôtel Le Cep in Beaune and Abbaye de La Bussière in La Bussière-sur-Ouche.

SPAIN
Sierra Nevada

SARAH WOODS

After a couple of days of blissful cycling through gently climbing foothills and slopes, it will take a while for the slow-burning pain in your calves to fully register on your radar. In warm Spanish sunshine, you will breeze along for an entire weekend feeling more than a little smug at the ease with which you progress. By the end, however, you will have developed a pathological hatred for your saddle, once relatively comfortable but now an instrument of torture. You will also be suffering from rather peculiar hazy hallucinations no doubt prompted by the altitude. After navigating a succession of Volvo-sized potholes,

▽ *The view of Pico Veleta from the Poqueira Refugio.*

△ Passing under Mulhacen on the way to Pico Veleta.

you'll be seriously tempted to sell your soul for just a few metres of asphalt. The Sierra Nevada's legendary debilitating fatigue will already be kicking in, and bits of you will be purple, red and blue: bruised, raw and saddle sore.

Give up? Not a chance, as these aching limbs are well worth the rewards of two-wheeling the highest peak in Spain. A picnic of chorizo, olives, bread and cheese will help to revive your flagging spirits as you pedal on high into the Sierra Nevada, leaving the steamy 36°C (97°F) humidity-laden summer behind in favour of the clouds. Here it's a glorious 25°C (77°F), with no wind to speak of. There isn't much oxygen either at 3,000 m (9,840 ft), so once the adrenaline thrill of reaching the top subsides, an overwhelming sense of fatigue kicks in. Altitude can also play havoc with your emotions, co-ordination and judgement, so it's best not to make any big, life-changing decisions at the peak.

Like many other cyclists before you, limber up on the valley slopes from the village of Capileira, the topmost settlement in the Poqueira Gorge. Picture-postcard wooden beamed, whitewashed Alpujarran houses topple over narrow, winding streets. A road hemmed by varicoloured pot plants climbs out of the village and looks out over pepperpot chimney rooftops to provide a stunning opening panorama. Push the pedals to pass cacti and lush, leafy vegetation before things toughen up and the road is swallowed up by piles of crumbling rocks.

Accommodation is offered by way of the Refugio del Poqueira, where you may well join a civilized bunch of bearded outdoor-types to overnight at 2,500 m (8,200 ft). Over a sumptuous three-course meal of rabbit, complete with Andalucian wine, you'll swap tales of lunar-like dry river beds, forest trails and pea-soup fog – and relish every morsel. Thanks to the scrambling hooves of mountain goats and a relay of *contrabandistas*, the Sierra Nevada boasts more well-formed singletrack gully trails than you can shake an isotonic energy drink at – and all of it natural. A broad range of terrain ranges from sprouting farmland in the foothills through pine thickets to craggy barren peaks. Dry, dusty sinuous stretches dwindle to loosely scattered rocks in an instant, with steep sandy ravines and nailbiting drops. Tangled roots and gnarled knotty creepers weave through skinny ferns and scrub on the unworldly trail up to Veleta – the second highest peak in Spain at 3,396 m (11,139 ft) and a hellish climb along a chilly, windblown ridge where ledges of snow cling determinedly to sheltered crevices, even in August. Deeper drifts can force an undignified dismounting on the more dishevelled snow-crusted flanks,

facts and figures

DESCRIPTION: Exploring the foothills and slopes of Sierra Nevada.

ROUTE LENGTH AND DURATION: 90 km (56 miles), three days.

WHEN TO GO: Mid-June to mid-September.

SPECIAL CONSIDERATIONS: Mountain bike, minimum 25 litre rucksack, essential spares, and clothing (including cold-weather items), sunblock and energy bars are all required. At altitude the temperature can drop to 5°C (41°F) with light winds, so take warm gear.

MAPS: 1:40,000 Sierra Nevada Tourist Map (www.penibetica.com)

TOUR OPERATORS: Biking Andalucia (www.bikingandalucia.com).

PERMITS/RESTRICTIONS: None.

ACCOMMODATION: Poqueira Refugio (www.madteam.net/refugios/1.Poqueira)

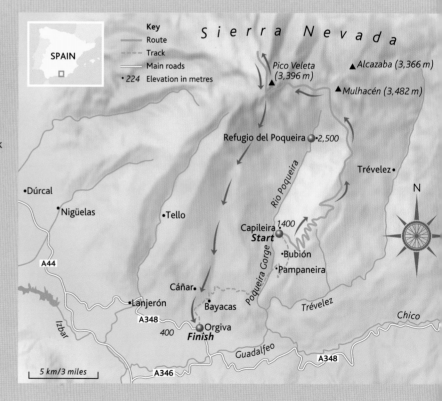

making it easier pride-wise to get off and walk. Then it's a steady slog up through jagged, rock-scattered mayhem to Pico Veleta, where jaw-dropping views produce an involuntary intake of breath – all of it bug-free. It is here that your body should finally be used to the jolts and jars in the saddle – or has given up protesting about it, at least. Imbibe the fragrance of damp mist and forest, gulp down several bottles of water and drink in the all-consuming quiet.

Next, it's an epic 3:1 vertical descent at eye-popping velocity through the wilderness to Orgiva – not something for anyone who's gravity-shy. Picking a line between the rocks requires brow-furrowing concentration while hurtling through a 19 km (12 mile) desert of boulders, rock and shale – an exhilarating heart-pumping fast-paced downhill thrill at speeds of 40 kph (25 mph). This is an unforgettable ride – the Sierra Nevada springs to life in the summer as wild flowers and herbs sprout up to fill the air with colour and scent, and tiny whitewashed weather-beaten villages hug the mountainsides while vultures and eagles swoop and soar in the thermals overhead.

▽ *Taking a break at the Laghuna Caldera.*

SPAIN
Camino de Santiago

TOM ROLLETT

Trekked by foot-sore pilgrims for over a thousand years, the Camino de Santiago across northern Spain is now one of the world's most awesome bike rides. This is a journey of extremes; from the snow-capped Montes de León, often impassable in winter, to the arid plains of the Meseta, where vultures and eagles swoop menacingly in the clear blue sky as the mercury edges towards 40°C (104°F). The views are stunning, the cities of Burgos, León and Santiago are buzzing with life, and even the most hardened atheist will be awed by the region's magnificent churches and cathedrals.

Accommodation *en route* is plentiful, ranging from basic refuges to grand palaces, including the oldest hotel in the world. While it pays to book ahead in high season, the beauty of biking this trail is that you can cycle until you're tired, and if one hostel is full, there's always another one just down the road. The ancient way of St James followed by hikers and horse riders is well signposted by yellow arrows, and much of it can be attempted on a hybrid or mountain bike. But there's always a metalled road nearby, making it suitable for road bikes too. Allow nine days to two weeks for this trip, depending on how fit you are and how much you want to sightsee.

Starting in Burgos, which is easily reached by a combination of plane, ferry, train or coach, you should leave the city via the cycle track on the N120, where you will begin crossing the dusty plains of the Meseta. The terrain is flat and the riding is easy, but temperatures can soar in summer. Pack a picnic and plenty of fluid – water and food can be hard to find. The huge skies and the peaceful isolation as you eat up the road make up for any hardship. This is a remote region, so when you do find a bar or restaurant it's worth making the most of it. Order a beer or a glass of Rioja, and tuck into local staples such as *patatas bravas* (spicy potatoes), cured meats, roasted peppers and of course the ubiquitous *tortilla* (Spanish omelette).

On through Castrojeriz, Fromista and Sahagún and then, some 210 km (130 miles) after setting off, you arrive at the bustling city of León. Take care as you enter the city limits, as the traffic will shock after the empty plateau and rustic villages you have left behind. Check out the cathedral's famous stained glass windows, stroll round the atmospheric old quarter – home to some of the region's best tapas bars – then blow your budget staying at the Hostal San Marcos. Behind the spectacular façade of this former monastery lies a 16th century church and cloisters.

Next day, continue through golden wheatfields to the Roman town of Astorga, but be sure to have a rest here and a strong *café con leche* at one of the streetside cafés before you set off, because now the climbing begins in earnest. The road steadily rises 650 m (2,132 ft) as it winds up the Montes de León, and if you don't stop for a breather you should at least pause and admire the fabulous views of the valley below. Just shy of the top, and just after the eerily abandoned village of Foncebadón, is the Cruz de Ferro, a giant cross erected on an ancient and still growing pile of rocks. For hundreds of years pilgrims have brought stones from home and, to signify the unloading of their sins, deposited them here. It's an impressive and moving sight.

Bomb down the other side of the mountain, but be sure to slow down for villages such as El Acebo, whose cobbled streets have claimed cyclists' lives in wet weather. At the bottom is the picturesque village of Molinaseca, where in summer the River Meruelo is

▽ *The village of O Cebreiro marks the peak of one of two mountain ranges you will cross.*

DESCRIPTION: From Burgos across the dusty Meseta to León, then over two mountain ranges, the rolling hills of Galicia and on to Santiago de Compostela.

ROUTE LENGTH AND DURATION: 540 km (335 miles), nine days.

WHEN TO GO: The mountains are impassable in winter. May–September are the best months, although the Meseta is baking hot in August.

SPECIAL CONSIDERATIONS: Take a road, hybrid or mountain bike. There are extremes of weather in the mountains and on the Meseta, so always check conditions and follow local advice. Galicia is notoriously wet, so take waterproofs. English is not widely spoken, so learn some Spanish! Check out the fantastic bike shop Bicicletas Velocipedo, Rua de San Pedro 23, Santiago de Compostela. They will box your bike for your flight back and even arrange a taxi to take you and your bike to the airport.

MAPS: Michelin maps 575 and 571.

TOUR OPERATORS: There are many, including Sarajan Tours, Easy Rider Tours and Saddle Skedaddle.

PERMITS/RESTRICTIONS: Religious travellers can get a Pilgrim Passport stamped along the way, giving access to cheap accommodation.

ACCOMMODATION: Huge range of hostels/hotels *en route* to suit all budgets. When you're finished, treat yourself at the five-star Hostal dos Reis Católicos.

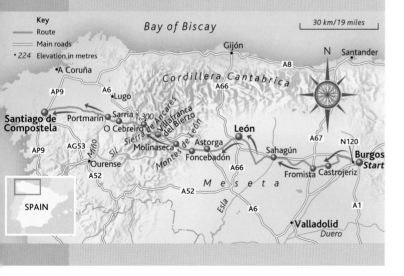

dammed to provide a natural swimming pool amid breathtaking beauty. Vineyards cloak the rolling hills as you approach the idyllic town of Villafranca del Bierzo, deep in wine country. Rest up with a glass of something cold and enjoy spectacular views of the Ancares mountain range, because once again it's time to climb.

Setting off from Villafranca, some four or five hours of arduous pedalling in first and second gear – this is a dangerous ascent to attempt in bad weather – will bring you to O Cebreiro, a tiny village at 1,300 m (4,264 ft). High in the Cantabrian mountains, it comprises around 12 thatched buildings, or *palozzas*, some of which date

back to the Bronze Age. Cross the summit and set off down the mountains, enjoying a well-deserved brake-burner down to Samos.

Push on through pine and eucalyptus forests to Sarria and then Portmarín, a rebuilt town moved stone by stone when its valley was flooded to construct a reservoir. The hot plains and mountain ranges have been replaced by the rolling green Galician countryside, and in this notoriously wet region you might find that the rain in Spain is falling mainly on you and your bike. The verdant hills provide a superb backdrop to the last leg of your adventure, though, and Santiago is now within touching distance.

Finally, after 540 km (335 miles) of cycling, you arrive in Plaza del Obradoiro. Here, Santiago's famous cathedral, housing the remains of Jesus' cousin St James, stands next to the Hostal dos Reis Católicos, reportedly the oldest hotel in the world. It is a spectacular square, one of the jewels in Spain's crown, and offers a fitting end to this incredible journey.

△ *Santiago's famous cathedral marks the end of the journey.*

△ ABOVE LEFT *The rolling green hills of the Galician countryside.*

ITALY
The Amalfi Coast

BEN LAURANCE

Some cycle rides are great because they allow you to get to wonderful places. Some are great because they offer the challenge of steep climbs and thrilling descents. But the ride along the Amalfi Coast is great simply because the road itself is so spectacular – a tarmac ribbon clinging to cliffs high above the azure waters of the Mediterranean, a dramatic, winding route through one of the most beautiful parts of Italy. Cycling the Amalfi Coast, running from Salerno to Sorrento, provides a flavour of Campania, the gateway to the Italian south, the *mezzogiorno*. Its natural beauty and calm provide the perfect antidote to the urban, bustling sprawl of Naples just up the coast. And it gives breathtaking views as the road climbs along the cliffside.

▽ *Houses cling to the cliffs leading down to the Mediterranean Sea.*

Salerno, at the start of the ride, is a bustling but rather charmless port city. Much of the centre was destroyed during an Allied landing in September 1943, but an old medieval quarter survives as did the city's architectural highlight, the enormous church or *duomo*, which dates from the 11th century. The city gives little hint of the beauty and drama of the coast to its west, but once you head out along the road towards Amalfi, leaving the port far below, the traffic begins to die down and the sight of the coast opens up. Cetara is an attractive, quiet fishing village worth a visit.

On this first day of the trip, the climbing is not strenuous, and Positano, the natural place to stop, is only 43 km (27 miles) away. For those with the stamina and inclination, however, there is the option of turning off the coast road and heading north for a detour to Ravello. There isn't much to the town itself – there's an 11th century church that was renovated in 1786, and the remains of Villa Rufolo, whose gardens are used for open-air concerts during the summer – but at 335 m (1,099 ft) above sea level and on the side of a mountain, Ravello offers an unrivalled view of the area. Andre Gide described it as "closer to the sky than to the seashore". For cyclists who enjoy steep climbs, the detour to Ravello is worthwhile simply for the perspective it gives on the whole Amalfi Coast.

Back on the coast road itself, the route takes in the town of Amalfi, once an independent republic, and a century ago discovered by the English upper classes as a pleasant spot to spend their winters. The town sits in a broad cleft of the coastline and now has the feeling of a prosperous and fashionable resort. The road continues, hugging the cliffs through patches of land that – against all the odds, given the steepness of the terrain – have been tamed by farmers for growing fruit. The roadside is peppered with stalls selling fruit and drinks, and there are several shops selling the region's distinctive ceramics.

At the end of the first day, you'll arrive at Positano. It is one of the most photographed towns in Italy – and with good reason. Its houses, painted in white and soft pastels and draped in bourgainvillea, cascade down the cliffside to the waters of the Mediterranean below. Positano's main cultural treasure is Chiesa de Santa Maria – try to get a view of it from above when the sun is out and reflecting off the church's extraordinary ceramic-clad

▽ *Make sure your camera is at the ready for the beautiful town of Positano.*

DESCRIPTION: A two day ride along one of the most spectacular coastal roads in Europe.

ROUTE LENGTH AND DURATION: 77 km (48 miles), two days.

WHEN TO GO: Avoid July and August and most weekends; weekdays in spring or autumn are ideal.

SPECIAL CONSIDERATIONS: Any road bike will do; low gears are useful for the hills. The road has very little shade, so take plenty of water and sun protection in warm weather.

MAPS: Touring Club Italiano 200,000:1 map of Campania and Basilicata is sufficient, or any other map of similar scale.

PERMITS/RESTRICTIONS: None

ACCOMMODATION: There are plenty of hotels at Salerno and Sorrento. Hotels in Positano are heavily booked, so make reservations or camp at Praiano, 5 km (3 miles) east of Positano.

dome. Positano has several hotels, or there is a campsite, La Tranquilita, about 5 km (3 miles) to the east at Praiano. The cheaper hotels in Positano are often booked well ahead, so making a reservation is essential.

Day two of the route is more strenuous, but no less rewarding than the first. The day's ride covers just 34 km (21 miles), but involves some long climbs along the cliff and through olive groves. The main road, the SS145, cuts across the peninsular to Sorrento, but instead stick to the quieter coast road to take in the pleasing old town of Massa Lubrense and the village of Termini. At Termini, leave your bike on the road and walk to the top of the hill to enjoy ravishing views across the Gulf of Naples and out to the island of Capri.

Then drop down into Sorrento – a town that's quite unashamed about being an out-and-out tourist resort. Like Salerno, Sorrento is not a place with many attractions for the independent traveller – it is the road joining the two places that provides the thrill. For the cyclist it is one of the greatest rides in the world, and a fabulous conclusion to this beautiful route.

184

◁ *Day two involves some long climbs, so enjoy the downhills when they come.*

▽ BELOW LEFT *Cafés and the cathedral in Amalfi.*

▽ *Atrani, near Amalfi, is another beautiful spot in which to take a break.*

GREECE
Crete

ROBIN GAULDIE

▽ *Remember to take sunblock and plenty of water when cycling in Crete.*

Crete is the largest and most spectacular of Greece's islands, with a series of mountain ranges rising steeply from its rugged coastline to heights of well over 2,000 m (6,560 ft). The Amari Valley is one of the island's better kept secrets. Well off the main beaten tourist track, it is a favourite with cyclists, cutting across the narrowest part of Crete from the north coast near the old Venetian town of Rethymnon to the Libyan Sea.

This route follows modern asphalt roads, but there is very little traffic once you leave the outskirts of Rethymnon and the busy coastal highway. Along the way, you will pass at almost every bend what look like doll's house-sized Greek churches, mounted on posts at the roadside. These are *iconostases*, erected in thanks to the Virgin Mary or to a patron saint by drivers who have had a narrow escape – or by the families of those who failed to negotiate one of the region's lethal bends. The first stretch takes you from not far above sea level to the watershed of the Sfakoriako watercourse, around 450 m (1,476 ft) above sea level. This is the most demanding stretch of the route, but has spectacular views of the Psiloritis massif to the northeast. Rising to a height of 2,456 m (8,056 ft), this is the highest mountain range in Crete. The road zigzags for around 8 km (5 miles), following the south side of Sfakoriako gorge, with steep drops in places. Opposite the gorge, terraced slopes dotted with patches of juniper, wild figs and small olive groves descend to the rocky bottom of the valley.

After the village of Prasies, the road continues to climb for some 16 km (10 miles), still following the Sfakoriako to its source close to the village of Apostoli. Just before you reach the village, a stone statue of an idealized *pallikar* (Cretan warrior) commemorates fighters of the Cretan resistance to the German occupation of 1941–45. In late 1944, German soldiers destroyed almost every village in the Amari region, which had been a hotbed of resistance activity ever since the German invasion. This is why so many of the villages you will pass through on this route look incongruously modern, having been rebuilt as recently as the 1960s.

At Apostoli, you can take a breather – it's not quite all downhill from here, but the most

△ *Good roads and lovely views make this an excellent ride.*

△ *Enjoy the downhills while they last!*

▷ *Roadside shrines, or* iconostases, *are erected by grateful survivors of near misses, or in memory of those who didn't make it.*

▽ OVERLEAF *The scenery along this route is stunning – be sure to take a camera.*

demanding ascent is now over and the general trend of the road is downward all the way to the south coast. From Apostoli, carry on for around 1 km (0.6 miles) to Agia Fotini. It's here that the valley begins to open out before you, revealing a surprisingly lush vista of fields, farms, meadows and olive groves that contrasts sharply with the almost lunar landscapes of the Psiloritis range to the northwest and the lower, but equally rugged, Kedros massif to the southwest. Over millennia, winter rains have washed every scrap of topsoil from the higher ranges into the valley below, creating a mountain oasis with soil that is – by Cretan standards – deep and rich. From April until mid-May, huge purple thistles, swathes of white and yellow daisies, purple vetch and scarlet poppies colour the fields, road verges and especially the pastures at the fringes of the valley.

Flocks of sheep and goats straying, or being herded, along the road are an occasional hazard of the Amari, and it's a good idea to keep one ear open for the brazen sound of goat bells ahead.

Detour left about 1 km (0.6 miles) after Agia Fotini to ride a further 1 km (0.6 miles) uphill to Thronos. Dump your bike next to the 14th century church in the centre of the tiny village, and walk about 800 m (2,624 ft) on a well-marked path to the site of ancient Syvritos. Archaeological excavations are still going on here, and it seems that the site was inhabited from the late Minoan era (12th century BC) until around the 4th–5th century AD. The ancient city covered the whole hillside, and painstakingly built cobbled roads ran the length of the Platis River gorge, connecting it with what's now Agia Galini on the south coast – trails that were still in use well into the second half of the 20th century.

Freewheel back to the main road and turn left, then carry on for around 5 km (3 miles) until you reach what by Amari standards is a major crossroads and spot signs directing you to Moni Asomaton. Founded more than 1,000 years ago, this Byzantine monastery is now deserted and a little spooky. The monastery grew rich and powerful by paying lip service to the Ottoman conquerors of Crete from the 17th to the 19th century, while secretly funding the struggle for independence. Like many Orthodox monasteries, its lands were expropriated by the Greek state in the 1930s and turned into a centre for agricultural research. The old monastery buildings stand empty and derelict, overshadowed by overgrown planes and palm trees, next to the more functional modern buildings of the agricultural college. Around it are the fields and lush meadows of the most fertile part of the Amari valley.

Return to the junction, cross over the main road and detour uphill, through Monastiraki village, to Amari, the main village and administrative centre of the valley region. A Venetian clocktower dominates the village, and is one of the few secular buildings in the region to have survived the ravages of the German army during World War II.

Return to the main road, turn right and continue for around 10 km (6 miles) through Vizari, where the road turns sharply to the east, and on to Fourfouras. This small village is the jumping-off point for the eight hour trek to the summit of Psiloritis, and is better supplied with places to eat and drink than anywhere else in the area. From here, the road winds quite gently through the southern fringes of the valley, with the steep slopes of Psiloritos looming on your left, through the villages of Kouroutes, Nithavris and Apodoulou, then turn right to Mandres. Immediately south of Mandres, turn right on the main coast road and freewheel downhill for some 8 km (5 miles) to the small resort of Agia Galini, where chilled beer, hot showers, and the prospect of an evening swim brighten the last few miles of the ride.

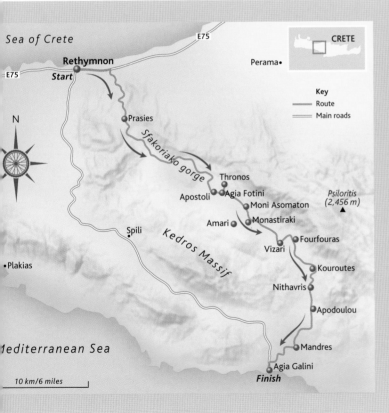

DESCRIPTION: A beautiful route that takes you across the narrowest part of Crete from the north coast near the old Venetian town of Rethymnon to the Libyan Sea.

ROUTE LENGTH AND DURATION: 56 km (35 miles). Allow eight hours.

WHEN TO GO: The best time to do this route is early May, when fields, roadside verges and hillsides are ablaze with wildflowers and daytime temperatures are around 20–25°C (68–77°F). Avoid November–March, when the weather is often cool, wet and windy.

SPECIAL CONSIDERATIONS: Road or mountain bike required. Take plenty of water and energy snacks. There are small tavernas and shops in some of the villages along the way, but opening times are irregular.

PERMITS/RESTRICTIONS: None.

ACCOMMODATION: Agia Galini, at the end of this ride, has plenty of small guesthouses and hotels and numerous bars, restaurants and cafés.

INDEX AND PICTURE CREDITS

PICTURE CREDITS

Rob Ainsley: pp74–75; Alf Alderson: pp79, 86, 87, 89 (r), 90–91; Martin Arpon: p127; Andrew Bain: pp66–73; Ian Benford: pp94–97; Helen Bevis: pp160–61, 163 (t); Biking Andalucia (www.bikingandalucia.com): pp174–77; Brylliantimages: pp162 (l), 162–63 (b); Adam van Bunnens/Alamy: p182; Butterfield & Robinson: pp170, 172–73; Jan Csernoch/Alamy: p99; Carole Edrich: pp65, 92, 109, 118–26; F1online Digitale Bildagentur GmbH/Alamy: pp190–91; FAN Travelstock/Alamy: p187, 188; Robin Gauldie/www.sargasso-travelimages.com: p189; Tim Greening: pp19, 20–21; Christopher Griffin/Alamy: p185 (t); Lars Halbauer/dpa/Corbis: p183; Gavin Hellier/Robert Harding World Imagery/Corbis: pp89 (l), 184; Hemis/Alamy: p101; Jeremy Hoare: pp62–64; Gavin McDonald: pp15, 17, 18 (r); Robin McKelvie: p157; Jacques Marais: pp1–13, 14, 22–28, 78, 80–85, 148–55; Mediacolors/Alamy: p186; Adam Monaghan: pp130, 136–41; Edrich Pardo: pp108, 110–13; Steve Razzetti: pp16, 18 (l), 30–61; Realimage/Alamy: p100; Carmen Roberts: pp104–07; Emiliano Rodriguez/Alamy: pp128–29; Tom Rollett: pp178–81; Ian Shaw/Alamy: p171; Jon Sparks: pp142–147, 156, 158–59; Paul Springett/Alamy: pp102–03; Vince Streano/Corbis: p185 (b); David Wall/Alamy: p77; Richard Wareham Fotografie/Alamy: p98; Max Wooldridge: pp131, 164–69; Luke Wright: pp93, 114–17; Yorkshire Dales National Park Authority: pp132–35.